We Preach Christ Crucified

WE PREACH CHRIST CRUCIFIED

KENNETH LEECH

Church Publishing, Incorporated
New York, New York

A catalog record for this book is available from the Library of
Congress.

ISBN: 0-89869-499-X

Acknowledgments
The extract from 'Friday Morning' on p. 18 is reproduced from
'Green Print for Son', Sydney Carter © 1960, 1969 Stainer & Bell
Ltd.

Biblical quotations are from the *New Revised Standard Version*
unless otherwise stated.

I have referred to the Common Eucharistic Lectionary, as used in
most Roman Catholic, Anglican, and Lutheran churches throughout the world, when referring to public readings from the scrip-
tures during Lent and Holy Week. I have kept references to other
works to an absolute minimum.

Printed in the United States of America.

Church Publishing, Incorporated
445 Fifth Avenue
New York, New York 10016

Contents

Preface

This book is based on a series of my Holy Week sermons and first appeared in the United States in 1995. It is still being reprinted over a decade later and a Japanese edition has just appeared. *We Preach Christ Crucified* differs from my other books in that it is shorter, and in that I have retained, as far as possible, the preaching style. While I believe strongly that every sermon is unique and is preached to and within the context of a particular community, my sense is that the fact that this book grew from preaching enabled me to speak through it to many people in a way not unlike that of an actual sermon. My impression too is that this book is read by people to whom my other books do not appeal.

I have, over many years, spent a long time grappling with both the preaching of the cross and the cruciform character of Christian life. It is, of course, essential to try to communicate the Christian life as a whole as a putting on of Christ, a sharing in his dying and rising. However, like most Christians, I continue to struggle with what this means in our daily lives and in our theological praxis. Again, my impression is that many readers have used this book as one that they can read and re-read, an impression reinforced by several reviewers.

After the book's first appearance, I attended numerous Lent groups around the United States where congregations were studying it. I was struck by the number of people who told me that it had led them to pray, and that they had struggled with and meditated on the chapters, often paragraph by paragraph. Wherever I travelled it was always the same two of the six chapters that puzzled, confused, or troubled people: chapters three and five. One is a chapter in which I tried to look at the politics of the cross, while the other deals with the darkness that is central to faith. Many Christians find it difficult to look at the cross politically, partly because we have individualised and spiritualised its meaning, partly because politics has itself fallen into disrepute. For many, too, the idea that faithful Christians should experience darkness is hard to take: a stress on joy, light, and assurance has associated such areas as doubt, inner turmoil, and the 'dark night of the soul' with sin and failure rather than being seen as essential elements in the life of faith.

This little book is important to me for another reason. The tendency for theologians to speak only to one another in a language that at times becomes impenetrable to those outside the academy has always worried me. I hold strongly to the belief that the theologian must preach the gospel in its depth and its simplicity, and that regular contact with 'ordinary people' within the common life of the church is essential. I found the example of the Chicago-based theologian David Tracy helpful here. Although Tracy is often seen—and rightly seen—as a complex theological writer, I was struck by his ability to preach to congregations on the South Side of Chicago in the most simple language and yet with great profundity. I do not think that there is any future for theology apart from this kind of rootedness among the people.

Augustine says that Christ is present among those who are 'in severe trial', and goes on to say that 'we progress by means of trial'. No one knows himself except through trial'. How true that is. The cross is about being broken. Many years ago I worshipped in a 'storefront church' in the London docks, and one of our favourite hymns was 'Jesus, keep me near the Cross'. The chorus is:

In the Cross, in the Cross,
Be my glory ever
Till my raptured soul shall find
Rest beyond the river.

A large West Indian lady, known by all of us as Aunt Matilda, always sang 'ruptured' instead of 'raptured', and her voice was so powerful that the whole congregation followed her. Yet in a way she was right. The cross does involve a rupture, a break, a cleavage. It is a moment of division and disturbance, a point of crisis, a breaking point.

There are two other aspects of the proclamation of the cross that have been important, at least to me, since this book first appeared. The first is the remarkable revival in many places, not least in Latin America, of the Stations of the Cross, a way of entering into the Passion journey which involves visual art as well as dramatic action. The Stations are a discipline of following the human, suffering Jesus, a discipline which aids discipleship. In her commentary on her own remarkable Stations hanging in Christ Church, Eastbourne, the artist Beverley Barr writes:

Most of the Stations I've seen gloss over Christ's suffering, and show an Arian Jesus swooning elegantly, and, at the deposition, one feels that a good dose of *sal volatile* will soon bring him round. Mine would not be like that. I felt that we do him little credit if we underplay his sufferings, nor do we do ourselves any favours that way, since how can we recognise that he is with us in our anguish, when we patently feel that he didn't actually suffer for real.[1]

What Beverley sought to communicate through her visual work is exactly what I tried to do in this book: to locate the cross within the context of the human Jesus and our own humanity. I hope very much that her Stations will be made available to a wider audience, for so much good theology is communicated through art and colour, rather than through the spoken or written word.

The second aspect, which I emphasised in the book, is the centrality of the cross not only in preaching and liturgy, but also in pastoral care. Since I wrote, Sharon Thornton's remarkable book *Broken Yet Beloved: a pastoral theology of the Cross* has appeared.[2] It makes the point very strongly that the cross is critical to pastoral theology, although she also claims, rightly in my view, that the cross has been seen in conventional Christian terms as belonging within the sphere of doctrine, not that of 'pastoralia'. Like Thornton, I want to reject this false division. The cross is indeed central to Christian faith, life, ministry, and discipleship. I hope that the new edition of this little book will help to make that clear.

—KENNETH LEECH
APRIL 2005

1. Beverley Barr, *Stations of the Cross at Christ Church, Eastbourne,* privately published. The Stations can be viewed on the Internet at www.xpeastbourne.org.
2. Sharon G Thornton, *Broken Yet Beloved: a pastoral theology of the Cross* (St. Louis, Missouri: Chalice Press, 2002).

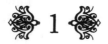

Foolishness
to the Greeks

For Jews demand signs and Greeks desire wisdom,
but we proclaim Christ crucified, a stumbling block
to Jews and foolishness to Gentiles, but to those
who are the called, both Jews and Greeks, Christ
the power of God and the wisdom of God.

(1 Corinthians 1:22–24)

STRANGE MEMORY

Thousands of people were crucified during the sixty-five years from the time that Judea became a Roman province until the end of the Jewish War. Almost all of them are now forgotten: they have become part of the immense historical mass of the anonymous dead. Such a loss of identity is hardly surprising in the aftermath of this most degrading and dehumanising form of punishment in which, according to Cicero, even the name of the victim should be removed. The rotting corpses were often left for vultures and animals to devour. It is this form of punishment, reserved mainly for the lower classes, particularly for slaves, violent criminals and instigators of revolt, which provides the location for these reflections on the work of our salvation.

Among the crucified people, Jesus of Nazarath alone is remembered. But he is not only remembered, he is remembered by his followers as the crucified God. The accounts of his death in the gospels are the longest and most detailed accounts of crucifixion in the whole of ancient literature, and the event itself is supported by evidence which is better than that for any similar event in the ancient world. Within the gospels themselves the accounts of the passion (suffering) and death of Jesus take up the largest single sections: indeed the gospels have been described as passion narratives with extended introductions. Clearly this crucifixion is seen as being exceptionally important, at least by some people.

Within the community of his followers, Jesus is remembered – in the most literal sense, re-membered. Week by week, day by day, in the eucharistic offering, in the exposition of the word and in other ways, there is a ritual re-enactment, an *anamnesis*, of the dying and rising of Jesus. It is the Eucharist or Mass – that regular act in which Christians claim to 'eat the flesh' and 'drink the blood' of Christ – which most dramatically manifests and makes present the mystery of the cross and resurrection. This ritual or liturgy is central to Christian consciousness and to the nurturing and sustaining of Christian identity. 'Do this in remembrance of me' stands at the heart of Christian worship. Yet it is a strange act and seems to the outsider to be a foolish one. For here Christians not only retell the ancient stories, they claim to re-enact the Last Supper, relive the sacrifice of Calvary and of heaven, and remember their own broken body through solidarity with the broken and glorious body of Jesus Christ. This 'unbloody sacrifice' of the Mass is strange, mysterious, fascinating and impenetrable, and, for all the attempts to dispense with its mystery and reduce it to a crude one-dimensional fellowship meal, the complexity of the mystery keeps returning. In the mystery of the Mass we are, as it were, present at Calvary and at the resurrection. It is a strange event rooted in a strange memory.

While most Anglican eucharistic prayers use 'remembrance', the English versions of the Roman Mass use the weaker word 'memory'. However, while memory is often seen as a looking back to past and finished events, in recent years there has been a renewed emphasis on corporate memory, the memory which recovers lost traditions and suppressed histories, the memory which nourishes and strengthens movements and struggles. Memory is of the greatest importance in the lives of Christians. Without memory there can be no forgiveness, no healing of the hurts and pain of the past. And forgiveness and healing are central to Christian existence. The trouble is that our memory is often blocked. Past hurts and sufferings are too painful to remember, so we blot them out of consciousness. We often justify this organised amnesia by saying that we 'live for the present'. But living for the present can easily be an evasion of the reality of our past. It is this evasion which must be undermined, lovingly yet deliberately, by the Christian community. For to live within a community of faith is to live within a community of memory, and the Christian community is shaped by what J. B. Metz calls 'the dangerous memory of the passion of Christ'. It is a community with a history. T. S. Eliot in 'Little Gidding' tells us that a people without history is not redeemed from time, and, in Christian thought, redemption takes place both within time and from the captivity of time.

However, the word 'remember' brings out the present dynamic in the past events. To re-member is to put together again. And this is what happens among the disciples of Jesus. Week by week, day by day, the Christian community celebrates the mystery of his dying, breaking bread in his memory, and in that fragmentation, that brokenness, celebrates its own unity as 'one body in Christ'. The term 'body of Christ' is used in Paul to mean both the Eucharist and the people. This continual memorial or *anamnesis* is more than an act of nostalgia. It is a putting together again of the body of Christ which was broken and given for the life of the world. There is something immensely powerful and energising about this movement, and yet we must admit that it is very odd, very strange – indeed, on the surface, utterly absurd. For one would have thought that the event of Calvary would have marked the end of what we call 'Christology', thinking about Jesus as the Christ, the Messiah: it would seem to mark the disastrous failure of a project. Yet this seems not to be so. Christ was broken and crushed, and yet it is when we are broken and crushed that we know him. Christ was a failure and it is in the midst of our failure that we know him, not as another failure but as a source of life and power.

In fact the original Calvary experience was, for the disciples, one of failure. It was later, on the road to Emmaus, and on similar subsequent encounters, that the reality of the cross and of the crucified one became a living reality. It was on the first Pentecost after the death of Jesus that, as a result of Peter's preaching, they were 'cut to the heart' (Acts 2:37). It was as a result of the preaching of the gospel of the crucified Christ that people were brought to faith and discipleship.

And so it has been through all the succeeding centuries. Although evidence suggests that friendship and the witness and examples of friends is the most important single factor in leading people to Christian faith, there is a power in preaching which is not dependent on the preacher's own ability or personal strength. We may be chained in various ways but the word of God is not chained (2 Timothy 2:3). There is liberating and healing power in the word. So the Letter to the Hebrews says that the word of God 'is living and active, sharper than any two-edged sword, piercing until it divides soul from spirit, joints from marrow' (Hebrews 4:12). Similarly the Baptist preacher C. H. Spurgeon, when he was asked 'Why do you defend the Bible?', replied, 'I do not defend the Bible. The Bible is a lion. Set it free and it defends itself.' In preaching, we are seeking not so much to draw attention to ourselves or our rhetorical and dramatic ability as to set free, to liberate, the word so that it does its own (or rather God's) strange work (Isaiah 28:21, King James Version).

GOD'S STRANGE WORK:
LIFE THROUGH THE CROSS

For his followers Jesus is the exact opposite of Humpty Dumpty. Not only is his broken life put together again in the resurrection, but each celebration of the

Christian community is a re-membering of Christ, a putting together of the Christ who was broken and smashed. But in this re-membering, we become his members, his body, the extension of his incarnation and passion into human history. It is in this social experience that salvation is found. For salvation involves a participation in a new history, becoming members of a new community. We are not redeemed in isolation but as part of a redeemed community, a community brought into being by God's strange work. When Christians meet together to break bread and share wine in his memory, they are taking part in an act which helps them to live. Through this act the distant figure from first-century Galilee and Jerusalem becomes a living presence and source of life.

The re-membering of Christ, the movement of his passion into human history, is one of the most striking, most baffling and yet most clear features of the human story. For when people contemplate this crucified figure, they do so not as a solitary and tragic martyr but as a source of strength and grace, and as a way of deepening solidarity in pain and struggle. To re-member Christ in his dying is to become his members, his limbs and organs, to be his body crucified and risen. It is to reawaken his memory as a contemporary source of strength and illumination. Or so Christians claim.

So in contemplating the passion, we look back to the event of Christ's death, not only as a historical memory, but as a source of life, of freedom, of nourishment, of renewal. In that crushed and broken victim, we see our hope, our only hope, in a world which continues to crush and break the children of God.

GOOD FRIDAY: THE FEAST OF FOOLS

Christians commemorate Christ's death on that paradoxical day called Good, a paradox which has been
reinforced twice in recent years by its coincidence with
April Fools' Day. It is a coincidence with deep meaning.
On Good Friday we celebrate the fact that 'God lets
himself be pushed out of the world on to the cross'
(Dietrich Bonhoeffer). It is the feast of the divine folly.
Indeed in the New Testament the cross is seen, and its
proclamation is seen, as an act of folly. St Paul puts it
like this:

> For the message about the cross is foolishness to
> those who are perishing, but to us who are being
> saved it is the power of God. For it is written, I will
> destroy the wisdom of the wise and the discernment
> of the discerning I will thwart ... Has not God
> made foolish the wisdom of the world? For since,
> in the wisdom of God, the world did not know
> God through wisdom, God decided, through the
> foolishness of our proclamation, to save those who
> believe. For Jews demand signs and Greeks desire
> wisdom, but we proclaim Christ crucified ... For
> God's foolishness is wiser than human wisdom,
> and God's weakness is stronger than human
> strength. (1 Corinthians 1:18–25)

Paul goes on to say that God has chosen what is foolish
in the world to confound the wise (1:27). And so if
anyone claims to be wise in this age, that person must
become a fool in order to become wise (3:18). The cross
is described as *moria*, insanity (1 Corinthians 1:18f.)

and as 'God's foolishness' (1:25). We need to become fools in order to become wise because the wisdom of this world is foolishness with God (3:18).

It is essential to grasp the importance of this idea of folly in sharing the mystery of the cross and in following the way of the cross. One of the earliest crucifixes shows Jesus with the head of an ass, an image which no doubt was derived from Paul's portrayal of the cross as folly. But we could say that the entire life of Jesus was an act of folly. There is no sense in it by worldly conventional standards: his solidarity with outcasts, his extreme demands, his polemic against the rich and devout, all culminating in his death as a rebel and criminal. It is quite unreasonable. Christ is a fool, a symbol of contradiction, of the foolishness of God. And those who follow his way become sharers in his folly. They become 'fools for the sake of Christ' (1 Corinthians 4:10).

Sadly it is only in the Eastern Orthodox tradition (and particularly in the Russian tradition) that the status of the holy fool is recognised liturgically and that folly for Christ's sake is seen as an integral part of spirituality, consciously celebrated and revered. The first saint to be recognised as a fool was St Simeon Salos, a Palestinian monk who died at the end of the sixth century. He threw nuts at the candles during the liturgy and ate sausages publicly on Good Friday. St Andrew the Fool walked naked through the streets of Constantinople and behaved as a beggar. The fools reappeared in thirteenth- and fourteenth-century Russia. The most famous of the fools of Russia, St Basil the Blessed who lived during the sixteenth century, made Tsar Ivan the Terrible eat raw meat, consorted with prostitutes, threw stones at the houses of respectable people and stole from dishonest traders. He too ate sausages on Good Friday and walked naked through the streets of Moscow. The fools were often nomads and pilgrims, always figures of the absurd. They appeared particularly during periods of complacency in Church and society. Essentially the holy fools kept alive the scandal of the naked, accursed saviour who was killed outside the camp.

In the west, the Cistercians maintained the tradition of folly for Christ's sake. William of St Thierry (1085–1148), in his book *The Mirror of Faith*, says that Christ's wisdom is mad and that Christians are called to 'holy madness' (*sancta . . . amoris insania*). Francis of Assisi was called to be a 'new fool' in the world, while Irish tradition is filled with accounts of wild and strange men who were possessed of deep perception and insight. Nor are the holy fools extinct. On Good Friday 1994 – also April Fools' Day – Father Carl Kabat, dressed as a clown, hammered on a Minuteman III missile in North Dakota, for which he was sentenced to five years in prison.

John Saward, whose work *Perfect Fools*[1] is the authoritative study of folly for Christ's sake in east and west, argues that the holiness of the fools shows itself most in their solidarity with the outcasts of society. They are not content with 'social work' but identify completely with the wretched of the earth. They see Christ present in beggars, lepers and prisoners, and particularly in moral and mental outcasts, whose behaviour makes them intolerable in conventional society and among the comfortably devout and pious. But the fool belongs also to the tradition of prophecy, and points to the madness and evil of a world system organised apart

St Teresa

from Christ, apart from love and mercy. So the fool stands in all ages as a scandal and an offence to respectable religion, stands as a constant and disturbing reminder of the Christ who was crucified outside the gate (Hebrews 13:12).

I believe that in some way we are all called to be fools for Christ's sake, and that the word of the cross will not make sense apart from this willingness to take the form of a fool. We come always before the cross as fools, as disciples of that messianic fool who entered Jerusalem on an ass and died in apparent failure as an act of supreme folly. Religion goes disastrously astray when it ceases to be a sign of contradiction and becomes the cement for social conformity. The foolishness of God is then replaced by capitulation to the values of the world. A Church which owes its origins to the cross cannot, if it is to be true to its nature, be the slave of worldly norms and stereotypes. Conformity to the world is the betrayal of its foundation in folly and contradiction, and of its necessary role as a community of contrast and of dissent.

So we are urged to be transformed, not conformed (Romans 12:2), an injunction which the Church seems constantly to be in danger of reading in reverse! The temptation to conformity and to 'rationality' recurs in every generation in different forms. The Church is urged to adjust, to 'come to terms with', the values and assumptions of the dominant culture instead of challenging and critiquing them in the name of the Jesus who came to bring a *krisis* to the world and its systems (John 12:31). The temptation to conformity must be resisted if the scandal of the Church under the cross is to be sustained.

THE SCANDAL OF INCARNATION
AND PASSION

There are many theories about how the saving work of Christ takes effect but none of them is quite satisfactory. None approaches the heart of the mystery which is best embodied in symbol and sacrament. The symbol of the dying Christ is both tragic and comic, terrible and, by conventional standards, ridiculous. It represents failure and foolishness. Yet out of this foolishness comes a strength and a source of wisdom which is beyond secular reason to comprehend. I do not mean by this that Christianity is fundamentally irrational. Clearly in order to take the step of faith in Christ at all one must believe that it is, in some sense, a 'reasonable' step to take. But as one moves closer to that which draws us and transforms us, it is mystery, not rationality, which takes over. In the end, it is faith and love, not thought, which attracts us to this strange figure on the cross.

And, in any case, we need to ask; whose rationality? There is no independent, 'objective' standard of reason which hovers conveniently over the world. Rationality emerges from and is embodied in particular traditions. In order to understand the power of the crucified Christ, we need to remember what it is that Christians, those who stand within this particular tradition, believe about him. Christian faith is not a reasonable set of beliefs for adults which suddenly goes mad and regresses to fantasy when it comes to the death on the cross. At the very core of the faith is the absurdity of the Word made flesh, God made small. As one Christmas carol expresses it:

O wonder of wonders, which none can unfold:
The Ancient of Days is an hour or two old;
The maker of all things is made of the earth,
Man is worshipped by angels, and God comes
to birth.

So scandalous and so amazing is this truth that it is
conventionally banished to the safe world of the Christmas card or crib. Christ is enclosed within the manger
where he can be controlled: he does not grow up, teach,
suffer, or die, or rise again in this Peter Pan theology.
Yet until we recover the scandal and mystery, as well
as the redemptive direction, of Christmas, we will not
make much sense of Good Friday and Easter. Christ,
Paul tells us, emptied *(ekenosen)* himself and took the
form of a slave. This theme of the 'emptying' *(kenosis)*
of Jesus is normally used as a way of talking about the
incarnation. But Paul immediately says that he then
humbled himself in obedience to this most extreme
form of death (Philippians 2:7). He endured crucifixion
as one who was in the form of God. So Christians have
dared to say that God was crucified. It was God who
hung there. If this is so, then in our relationship to the
cross, we are entering into something very close to
the mystery of God's being. All Christian claims must
have their focal point in the crucified Christ, in this
love-directed journey of God into the land of human
brokenness.

The idea of a crucified Messiah, a *Christos estauro-
menos* (1 Corinthians 1:23), was not known to earlier
Jewish theology. It would have been viewed as barbaric
and mad by most of those who listened to the message.
Yet the Christian claim was, and is, that our situation

was so dark, so hopeless, that God himself must enter it in order to transform it into light and liberation. 'God with us' in Christian understanding means the entry of God in the most specific and concrete way into human history. Bethlehem and Calvary, crib and cross, stand together. It is the Word made flesh who hangs on the tree. In the words of St Gregory Nazianzen: 'We needed a God made flesh, a God put to death, that we might live again.' Without this central gospel truth of God revealed in human flesh, the passion of Christ is meaningless. And yet this truth is not known by reason. It is grasped by an act of daring, of folly, of holy madness. It is an absurd and strange claim: that God poured himself out, became insignificant and small. And it is in the very strangeness, the insignificance and smallness, that we enounter the holy.

George Herbert in his poem 'The Sacrifice' brings out the ambiguity of the cross of Christ by his curious comparison of Jesus with a boy climbing a tree to steal fruit.

> O all ye who pass by, behold and see
> Man stole the fruit but I must climb the tree,
> The tree of life to all, but only me:
>   Was ever grief like mine.[2]

Christ incarnate, Christ crucified, hangs before us as a perpetual sign of the absurd, of the divine foolishness, a sign of contradiction in a world of 'sanity'. And all our theology, all our prayer and life, must begin with amazement, horror and wonder at the absurd mystery of the crucified God. Here the terrible gulf between humanity and God is experienced as a gulf *within* God.

And that is the point of revelation. 'When you have lifted up the Son of Man, then you will realise that I am he' (John 8:28).

So it is the task of the preacher to hold up Christ as a symbol of folly and scandal, a sign of contradiction, and so to bring about that *krisis*, that turbulence and upheaval in the soul which opens it to the word which is the power of salvation. At the core of the preaching of the cross is the sense of paradox. It is more important that the preacher has prayed, has been pierced by the word of God, and has become open to the activity of the Spirit, than that she has made elaborate and tidy preparation. None of us knows how God is going to use us, and we should not be too 'ready'.

So, in the face of reductionism and attempts to draw the boundaries of rationality at the current scientific perimeter, the gospel of the cross points to a knowledge rooted in an inescapable strangeness and mystery. It is towards this knowledge that the holy season of Lent calls us. It is intended to be a time of insight and of revelation through trial and contradiction.

LENT AS A TIME OF TRIAL AND CONTRADICTION

The season of Lent begins with the memory of finitude and mortality, the symbolism of dust. On Ash Wednesday, Christians are marked with the sign of the man of dust. Looking foolish, with ashes on our foreheads, we confront our own mortality in the midst of a culture which tries to deny death's reality. The mark of dust identifies us as foolish. Yet the sign is also the sign of the cross of the crucified and risen Christ, and so it speaks also of glory. Here too there is contradiction and contrast.

As Lent begins, the temptations of Jesus are set before us in the liturgy. Jesus goes into the wilderness, the place of desolation, of struggle, of trial. He enters not only the actual physical waste land but also the wilderness tradition of Israel, the world of temptation and trial, of Massah and Meribah, of murmuring and infidelity. The exodus of Jesus begins in the wilderness. And this too exposes the folly of his life. How much easier it would have been to succumb to those classic temptations. Jesus is shown as a human figure, one who wept and was tired, who hungered and thirsted. Yet the temptations are a microcosm not only of those which occurred throughout his life, relating to alternative understandings of God and of his vocation, but also of temptations which occur constantly in the life of Christ's disciples.

First, there is the temptation to turn stones into bread. Jesus is confronted by the temptation to acquire economic power, to choose the path of an economic provider, one who satisfies the demand for food and material provision. People would turn to him as the great provider. Against this he insists that human beings do not live by bread alone but by the word of God. The second temptation is to cast himself down, to perform a miracle, to assert spiritual power, using his spiritual resources to attract support and devotion and to manipulate people, to be a wonder worker. In response to this, he insists that spirituality is not about testing God but rather about testing our motives. Thirdly, Jesus confronts the temptation to acquire political power in exchange for idolatrous worship. He

could become a political autocrat. Against this he
asserts the absolute claim of the transcendent God.
Each temptation is a call to accept power.

Jesus recognises that power and rejects it as a personal possession. Instead he offers that power to a community, the community which is to be Christ spread
abroad and disseminated, a community which will be a
source of nourishment, a site for miracles, and a political force in the world. And in fact this is precisely what
the Church became within a short time: a storehouse
of both spiritual and material food; a place where great
and mighty wonders were seen; and a subversive force
which was to undermine the power of the Roman
imperium. So instead of turning stones into bread,
Jesus created a eucharistic community which offered
bread for the world. Instead of performing a miracle, a
spectacular display of power, he created a community
of spiritual power. And instead of seeking a dictatorial
imperialism, he created a community committed to
values of equality and sharing to work as a subversive
and transforming force within the structures of worldly
power.

Each of these temptations remains as a temptation
for us today. The Church has, over centuries, become
a storehouse of material things, a centre for distribution of food, clothing and material help for people
in need. There have been attempts by various Christian
communities to recover something of the *koinonia* or
common life of the Early Church. It is right that the
Church should take its role as material provider
seriously, and in order to do this we need to recognise
both the importance of bread to human life and
also the principle of 'not by bread alone'. We need,

particularly in the present climate of market-led capi-
talism, to beware of the danger of separating bread from
justice and equality, and becoming no more than a wel-
fare Church, exercising a soup kitchen and food pantry
ministry, the flip side of consumerism. We cannot offer
bread and then add a commitment to justice at a later
stage. The provision of bread alone can produce a
Church which colludes with the culture of possessive
individualism. The Russian philosopher Nicolas Berdyaev reminded us: 'Bread for myself is a material question; bread for my neighbour is a spiritual question.'[3]

The Church is easily seduced by the kingdoms of the
world so that it takes on their image, becomes an
imperium, a power structure, whose institutional form
is shaped by the prevailing secular hierarchical and
bureaucratic models and not by the gospel. Power
and stability come to matter more than truth. When
power is primary and the Church is seen as an end in
itself, the road to some kind of fascism is wide open.

The temptation to worship false gods is also an abid-
ing one. Lent is a time for scrutiny, for unmasking the
flawed consciousness which leads to idolatry. The mark
of dust is a reminder to us of the call to lowliness and
to the foolishness of the God whom the powers of
Church and State combined to crucify.

THE FOOLISHNESS OF GOD

The crucified God: it is either the most extraordinary
and wondrous truth, or the most bizarre blasphemy.
When Sydney Carter wrote his song 'Friday Morning',
with its refrain 'It's God they ought to crucify instead
of you and me', it was shunned by the BBC as anti-

religious! The song consists of words put into the mouth of one of the thieves crucified with Jesus.

It was on a Friday morning
That they took me from the cell,
And I saw they had a carpenter
To crucify as well.

You can blame it onto Pilate,
You can blame it on the Jews,
You can blame it on the devil –
It's God I accuse.

"It's God they ought to crucify instead
    of you and me",
I said to the carpenter a hanging on
    the tree.

The song ends:

"To hell with Jehovah!",
To the carpenter I said,
"I wish that a carpenter
Had made the world instead. . . ."

It is a song of holy folly, a song of contradiction. But it expresses in simple words the theology of the crucified God.

Good Friday, April Fools' Day. Christ dies as a fool, as a cursed one, one made to be sin for us. And we can only sit amazed. Only as fools for Christ's sake can we dare to call this Friday good.

Christian preaching and testimony is rooted in the

apparent absurdity, the foolishness of God, the foolishness of the cross. This preaching is not a controlled rational account of moral norms or theological propositions so much as a dangerous attempt to convey something of an experience of power and liberating grace flowing out of the heart of desolation and darkness. It is a proclamation, a lifting up, of the crucified Jesus as saviour and conqueror. Its power is inseparable from its paradoxical character. It is a mistake to try to eliminate, reduce or explain away the scandal and the offensive character of the cross. In the same way there is a paradoxical character about committed Christians, a strange and attractive combination of calm and unpredictability, of stability and surprise. Christian life is never a routine of foregone conclusions but is always open to the strange and the unexpected. As the fool disrupts the monotony of life, so the grace of God is subversive and destabilising in its strange work. Martin Luther King once described Christian people as 'creatively maladjusted', transformed nonconformists. Our task as holy fools for Christ's sake, creatively maladjusted to the wisdom of the world, is to hold fast to the folly of the crucified one, knowing that it is in his foolishness that our wholeness lies.

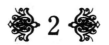

Healed by
His Wounds

By his wounds you have been healed.

(1 Peter 2:24; cf. Isaiah 53:5)

THE CROSS OF PAIN

The reality, the terrible and often unbearable reality, of pain and suffering, strikes at the heart of all religious belief. If Karl Marx was right to see religion as an opiate, a powerful pain-killer, then at least it can be seen to fulfil a 'transitional role'. At least it kills pain or makes it bearable. But the role of religion as analgesic, pain-killer, is not its only role. Often religion encourages its adherents to endure pain, to acquiesce in the role of patient sufferer. Often again it is religious belief which inspires and energises people to seek to end pain, to remove its causes, to attack its roots. And sometimes religion seeks to explain the origin and purpose of pain: and here it invariably fails.

The experience of Christ's death, and its expression in preaching, is not an explanation of anything: it is an announcement, a proclamation that, in this event, God has somehow entered into the pain of the world, has taken that pain into himself, and has thus created the climate in which pain can be transformed into a means of healing and an impetus to struggle for a world in which pain is ended and death itself is swallowed up. The proclamation of Christ's death involves an engagement with the wounded Christ, the Christ who suffers, who 'bears in his heart all wounds' (Edith Sitwell). If this engagement does not take place, the preacher is in deep trouble, and there is real danger of a descent into glibness and into that false sense of conquest which insults the sufferer and trivialises suffering. This glibness, rooted in the absence of any real engagement with the suffering of Christ, is instantly recognised by the hearer and is rightly rejected. The preacher, if he is to avoid this danger, needs to try, as best he can, to enter both into a profound solidarity and sympathy (or compassion) with Jesus Christ and also into the suffering of the people to whom he speaks. This solidarity and sympathy cannot happen if preaching is detached from prayer and from ongoing pastoral care.

Just as a glib and trivial exposition of the cross is recognised, so much of the power of effective gospel preaching comes from the fact that the preacher has, in prayer and in personal and social struggle, sought to enter into the reality of the pain of the world. For, while it is not the whole of the meaning of Calvary, the truth that we are healed by his wounds, and that God suffered in the flesh to heal the world, is a central truth with which we need to grapple throughout our lives. It is this encounter which motivates and energises our preaching, and without it, all preaching must end in failure.

EDITH SITWELL:
'STILL FALLS THE RAIN'

Nowhere in this century has the cosmic character of Christ's pain been expressed more powerfully than in Edith Sitwell's poetry, and particularly in her poem 'Still Falls the Rain'.[1] This poem surrounds the cross of nails in Pietermaritzburg Cathedral in Natal, South Africa, to which it was given by the people of Coventry Cathedral. Though its context is the air raids of 1940, it speaks to situations of violence today. In this poem the cross is seen as the manifestation of the pain of God, the pain of the air raids of 1940, and of thousands more nails since then. There are, Sitwell says, 'nineteen hundred and forty nails upon the cross'. The rain continues to fall at the feet of the starved man hanging there as the blood falls from his side. 'He bears in his heart all wounds.' As the poem reaches its climax, Sitwell sees Christ's blood streaming in the firmament, for this brow which we nailed to the tree holds the fires of the world. Through all the turmoil and violence he says: 'Still do I love, still shed my innocent light, my blood, for thee.' The rain of fire and earth gives way to the rain of divine grace and redeeming love.

'He bears in his heart all wounds.' That is the extraordinary and foolish Christian claim. It is a claim that God is in some way in the pain. In contrast to the character in Richard Jefferies' novel *Bevis* who exclaimed, 'If God had been there, he wouldn't have let them do it', the Christian gospel hangs on the belief that God *was* there, that God was at the heart of the pain and anguish, that the wounds were the wounds of God. God heals us by his wounds.

DISTORTED APPROACHES TO PAIN
AND SUFFERING

It is all too easy for those who have not suffered greatly to talk glibly about 'the redemptive power of suffering'. There is no guarantee that suffering will lead to lives of fulfilment, maturity and joyful surrender. The morbid and gloomy resignation which afflicts many religious people is not healthful and does not liberate. We see only too often the damage done by a self-destructive exaltation of what is wrongly called 'sacrifice', the scapegoat syndrome which is part of a wider victim mentality. A theology of self-sacrifice based on the cross can be particularly damaging to women who have often had lives of self-sacrifice thrust upon them, and for whom such a theology can reinforce the role of victim and the spirituality of self-hatred.

I can recall a member of a church who often spoke of her willingness to sacrifice herself for others. Not only was this her all-consuming aim in life, she had the wounds to prove it. She had sacrificed herself for her children, with the result that her children kept as far away from her as possible. Rarely smiling, her daily life was one of resigned cross-bearing, accompanied by sighs and self-inforced weariness. She had no interests, and felt guilty if she sat down, for the compulsive religion of self-sacrifice was totally engaging and demanding. She lived off her exhaustion, communicating it to others with intensity of infection. It could be said of her, as it was said of another person, 'She does good to others, and you can recognise the others by their hunted look.'

I also recall a clergyman who always seemed to

preach about the cross as 'Capital I Crossed Out'. The congregation got tired of this constant talk of crossing oneself out. The man himself had certainly crossed himself out and seemed to have no personality left. His sermons were gloomy and dismal, and did not present the cross as a source of energy and fulfilment, but rather as the morbid obsession of a diminished and damaged soul.

Such twisted religion has a lot to answer for. I believe it represents a serious misrepresentation of the cross and of the Christian response to pain. Instead of liberating the personality in the joyful service of God, this distorted idea of self-sacrifice results in dehumanised people, people without identity, without life, negated, driven, all but destroyed.

Linked with this masochistic element in religion is another, equally destructive trend: that towards a kind of paralysis which begins in guilt and ends in depression. Here our own guilt for sin and oppression becomes cosmic. We are so utterly crushed by the burden of guilt and by the apparently insoluble character of the world's sufferings that we are reduced to immobility. Imprisoned in guilt, our religion has ceased to set us free and reinforces our paralysed state. Nor is this simply a personal matter. Political grief can paralyse whole communities, making them unable to change or rebuild their lives.

On the other hand, suffering can be a creative response to pain, and we often see real maturity and holiness in the faces and lives of those who have been deeply wounded. By their wounds, we are healed. We often speak of 'the wounded healer', the person who is able to be an instrument of healing because of her own wounds and the way in which those wounds have been used. In my experience, many of those who have endured great pain and have transcended its damaging effects have a remarkable power to draw others to them when they are in need of strength and consolation. The great French spiritual guide Abbé Huvelin seems to have suffered from intense desolation, at times close to madness and suicide, yet out of this profound inner turmoil he was able to strengthen and direct others in the way of faith. God uses us in our weakness and woundedness, so that by our wounds others are healed. The message of the cross both to individuals and to communities must surely be a message that God has taken the guilt away, and has set us free to act for change through solidarity with the wounded Christ. He is the only scapegoat, and there is no need for more victims. He has died once and for all, *ephapax* (Romans 6:10; Hebrews 7:27; 9:12).

The late Audre Lorde, who died of cancer in 1992, made a distinction between pain and suffering which many have found helpful. Pain, she argued, was an event, an experience that had to be recognised, named and then used in some way in order for the experience to change, to be transformed into something else – strength or knowledge or action. Suffering, on the other hand, she saw as a kind of nightmare reliving of unscrutinised and unmetabolised pain. When people live through pain without recognising it, they rob themselves of the power that can come from using that pain, the power to fuel some movement beyond it. They thus condemn themselves to reliving that pain over and over whenever something close triggers it. That is what Lorde called suffering, a seemingly inescapable cycle.[2]

There is certainly nothing noble, nothing redemptive, about pain and suffering as such. Only within a framework of struggle for the liberation of self and of the creation (Romans 8), and of spiritual warfare against 'the powers' (Ephesians 6), can we can say suffering is part of the work of redemption. So in the midst of all the talk about 'orthodoxy' (right belief or right glory) and 'orthopraxis' (right action), we need to take very seriously Robert Schreiter's call for an 'orthopathema', a right way of suffering.[3] For real Christian faith is not morbid or masochistic, it does not glory in pain and suffering as ends in themselves. It sees that we are not victims, but that Christ is our victim. The Christian encounter with pain is an encounter which is realistic and which recognises the need to face the terrible reality of pain and yet to see and move beyond it. It is here that the preaching of the crucified God as the one who has gone before us as the pioneer (Hebrews 12:2) and leader of our struggle is of literally crucial importance.

THE SUFFERING GOD

A faith which seeks only to explain pain, and does not help people to share it and to overcome its destructive terrors, is a superficial faith which cannot carry us through experiences of profound anguish and desolation. In times of crisis it will be found wanting and cast aside. As Bonhoeffer said, 'only a suffering God can help'. It was the search for such a God which motivated Jurgen Moltmann when he returned from the prison camps, seeking a God who could help to make sense of that experience. He eventually wrote *The Crucified God*,[4] one of the most significant theological books of the twentieth century. Many people have said that without their faith in Christ crucified, life would be meaningless, its cruelty and suffering inexplicable and unbearable. That is why often the cross speaks to people and inspires people, comforts and transforms them, without their at all understanding what is happening. This is particularly true for many people who are sick and poor and who find in the crucified Christ a source of life and hope.

So at the heart of the life of the Christian community is the preaching of the crucified God. It is primarily an act of proclamation, not of elucidation. And this preaching is, at least, the proclamation that the healing of pain is a process within the heart of God; and that it is therefore a process which contains the seeds of victory. It is the rejection of a god who is beyond pain and feeling: the remote, impersonal 'god of the philosophers'. It is a rejection too of the belief that the world's pain is beyond healing. There must have been a Calvary in the heart of God before it was planted on the hill of Golgotha.[5] The need for the cross can only be located within the nature of God if that cross is to be truly redemptive. God could only have suffered on the cross if God was already that sort of God, a passionate, suffering God.

The idea of a suffering messiah does not seem to have been part of the main Jewish messianic hope. Certainly there is no clear text from pre-Christian Judaism which speaks of the suffering of the messiah. There is an idea in the Books of Maccabees that martyrdom has a saving value, and Eleazar is portrayed as one who gave his life to save the people (1 Maccabees 6:44), but there is nothing that comes close to the Christian idea except the 'suffering servant' theme in Isaiah 52–53. Here it is the servant of the Lord who suffers, not God himself.

To speak of the suffering God is dangerous language, and we need to beware of any tendency to glorify suffering and to forget that suffering is bad, that God is opposed to suffering and seeks to end it, and that Jesus was not abandoned but supported by God throughout the anguish of the passion and death. Yet, in spite of these qualifications, such language is demanded of us by the truth to which we bear witness. God on the cross means God in pain, God in distress, a suffering God. Only the suffering God can help.

From medieval times to the present there has been a stress on the importance of the physical wounds, the agony and the anguish, the human suffering of the human Jesus. St Bernard in his *Commentary on the Song of Songs* speaks of 'the richness of God's mercy in the open wounds of Christ'. Medieval crucifixes are often full of blood and mess, and the growing attention to the humanity of Jesus led to the devotions to the Sacred Heart and the Precious Blood. The *Anima Christi*, which dates from the early fourteenth century, prays: 'Within thy wounds hide me.' There is no doubt that this spirituality of the wounds has encouraged a harmful type of resignation and desire to escape the troubles of life. Many well-known hymns reflect this desire.

Jesu, grant me this, I pray,
Ever in thy heart to stay.
Let me evermore abide
In thy heart and wounded side.

Rock of ages, cleft for me,
Let me hide myself in thee.

Jesu, lover of my soul,
Let me to thy bosom fly . . .
Hide me, O my Saviour, hide
Till the storm of life is past.

Nevertheless we should not be too quick to condemn
or ridicule this need for comfort. There is an important
truth here about our need to trust in the blood, in the
achievement of Jesus, and not to go on wallowing in
unnecessary pain. Jesus came to remove burdens from
us, and it is an important task of the preacher to help
lift these burdens from people's backs and set them
free.

God bears in his heart all wounds. So desperate and
so dark is our situation that God must enter it if it is
to be transformed into a place of healing. The Christian
proclamation involves this and more. It is not just that
God was in the person of the wounded Christ but
that his wounds are our wounds, that he suffered and
died as our representative. So his pain is ours, our pain
is his. That is the point of Paul's tremendous claim: 'I
have been crucified with Christ . . . I carry the marks
of Jesus branded on my body' (Galatians 2:20; 6:17). It
is not that Jesus shows us the way and we are to imitate
him. The imitation of Christ is not a central theme of

the New Testament. Rather there is a solidarity in Christ, *en Christo*. Christ's cross is our cross, not because we are called to repeat it, but because he is our true identity, the eternal word, the light that enlightens us all.

The pastoral and spiritual importance of the suffering God is brought out by two contemporary writers. The Canadian theologian Douglas John Hall says:

> Until such a mutilated, sorrowful, forsaken Christ can be met in the churches of suburbia, there will be no facing up to the mutiliation, sorrow and forsakenness that this continent and its European satellites visit upon millions of the poor, including our own poor. Nor will there be any confrontation with the sickness within the soul of this society which causes it to seek the enemy outside its own soul.[6]

Writing in similar vein but at a more personal level, William McNamara, a Carmelite in Colorado, warns us that:

> Until the suffering God concept is understood and assimilated, not many people are going to enjoy passionate love affairs with God or live worldly lives of prayer.[7]

What Hall perceives in terms of social consciousness, McNamara sees in terms of personal spirituality. Neither will flourish unless there is a dynamic and profound encounter with the wounded and suffering God embodied in the crucified Christ.

SOLIDARITY AND TRANSFIGURATION

Once it has taken place, this encounter becomes itself a means of evangelism, for there is no surer way to Christ than through the example of transfigured people who have died and whose lives are hidden with Christ in God (Colossians 3:3). The power of God in the midst of affliction is shown both at Calvary and in the lives of human beings, those earthen vessels or 'clay jars' through which God's extraordinary power works. As a result, affliction does not lead to being crushed, nor does perplexity lead to despair, nor persecution to a sense of forsakenness, nor the fact that one is struck down mean that we are destroyed. Christians have a sense of hope in the midst of upheaval because we bear in our bodies the death of Jesus so that the life of Jesus may be made visible. Death which is at work in us produces life in others (2 Corinthians 4:10–11).

The cross of Christ then is not a call either to resignation in the face of unutterable pain or to a life of masochistic pursuit of suffering, often called 'the way of the cross'. It is a call to recognise solidarity with the Christ who has confronted pain and death once for all, and a call to minister to the wounded Christ as he is found broken and bruised on all the highways of the world. And here we see both the concrete significance and, in a profound sense, the irrelevance of Bethlehem and Calvary. Bethlehem and Calvary were the concrete, historic locations, the 'sites of significance', chosen of God and precious, the redeeming places. Yet Bethlehem is wherever there is no room; Calvary is all sites of cruelty and oppression. 'Just as you did it to one of the least of these . . . you did it to me' (Matthew 25:40).

It may now become clear why, with such a focus on suffering, we recall the transfiguration of Christ in Lent. (Indeed one small Christian body, the British Orthodox Church, actually celebrates the Feast of the Transfiguration during Lent.) On the Second Sunday of Lent, year by year, one of the accounts of the transfiguration of Christ from the synoptic gospels is read. Linked with the accounts of Abraham and a passage from Philippians, they recall us to the sense of this world as a place of pilgrimage and to the fact that our true homeland is in heaven. So we await the Saviour who will transform our bodies into the likeness of his glorious body (Philippians 3:17–4:1). The transfiguration is a message both about Jesus and about us. For in this moment Jesus is known for what he is. Yet all life is a process of discovery of our true identity and our potential for glory. Paul points out that, while our outer nature is wasting away, our inner nature – that is, our true nature – is being renewed daily (2 Corinthians 4:16). In focusing on the glory of God in the face of Christ we see also the potential glory of all people, however broken and degraded.

EDITH SITWELL:
'THE SONG OF THE COLD'

Thomas Merton saw the fact that there is 'no room' as a sign of the end, the end of human community, the end of responsible society, the end of care and of mercy. 'The time of the end is the time of no room.' So the inn at Bethlehem becomes the whole world, and in

the world, this 'demented inn', the poor, the damaged, the broken, are pushed further to the margins,
to the edge. They become insignificant, failures, non-
persons. They bear the stigma of rejection, the stigma
of the wounded Christ.

Many of us have witnessed, with deep sorrow and
horror, the growing cruelty and the loss of compassion
in our western culture. It has been aptly described as
a culture of contempt, an unprincipled society. Once
again it is Edith Sitwell, the poet who so powerfully
portrayed the wounds of Christ as reproduced in the
violence of war, who helps us to see the identity of
the wounded Christ with all those who are cast down
upon the highways of the world, those who are poor
and broken, and the judgement upon those who use
their wealth and status as a protection against seeing
Christ. Much of her poetry is inspired by the story of
Dives and Lazarus. The story is central to 'The Song
of the Cold' in which 'two opposing brotherhoods' in
the city are contrasted under the symbolic names of
Dives and Lazarus.[8] 'The falling night of the world
and heart' separates us from one another. People drift
aimlessly through the streets of the city with no homes,
'only famine for a heart'. Many die of the cold. But in
the night, Dives and Lazarus are brought together
under the cold's equality. The poem calls for compassion and for the recovery of human contact, and
ends with a desperate final prayer,

That I may weep for those who die of the cold –
The ultimate cold within the heart of man.

In 'The Shadow of Cain'[9] it is the theme of judgement

upon this society which is the dominant motif. Once again the context is 'the epoch of the Cold' where once there had been warmth in human veins. In the treatment of the poor, 'the Son of God is sowed in every furrow'. Again Lazarus appears as a symbol of the world's night, and to him are brought the condemned, the pitiable, the terrible, the loveless. Then Dives is brought, covered with the sores of gold. There is no warmth, no fire left in this condemned society. Yet each wound cries out more loudly than the voice of Cain. Sitwell warns that

> ... those ashes that were men
> Will rise again
> To be our fires upon the Judgment Day!

Sitwell's poems are much more relevant today when the social climate is marked by that increased polarising of rich and poor, and the political climate by that famine of the spirit, of which she wrote so powerfully. Today the pain of death itself is made more appalling by the fact that now more young people are dying. But there is also a polarising of consciousness, a breakdown in human relations, increasingly evident in the utterances of our political leaders. We have become the culture of which Edith Sitwell wrote, the culture devoid of human warmth, of compassion. 'The Song of the Cold' is the anthem of our society.

It is exactly twenty-five years since I started Centrepoint as an all-night shelter for homeless young people in the Soho district of London. Since then we have seen a massive increase, in both British and North American cities, in the numbers of young people forced on to the streets, more mentally ill people in the streets, more people dying, often literally of the cold. The change has been horrifying and yet what has been far worse has been the way in which so many of us have become acclimatised to the situation, innoculated against it. There has been a loss of passion, a loss of anger and of the impetus for change. The wounded Christ today is not crucified but ignored, dismissed as a statistic, or, when the tourists are offended, hose-piped away. As Studdert Kennedy wrote many years ago:

> When Jesus came to Birmingham, they simply
>   passed him by.
> They never hurt a hair of him, they only
>   let him die.[10]

At the same time there is no shortage of 'spirituality'. But we are being offered spirituality as another product on the market. Much of it lacks grief, struggle, rage and passion, those features which are so central to Sitwell's anguished writing and so central to the spirituality of the crucified God. Much contemporary spirituality lacks the imaginative encounter with poverty, pain and dereliction. It is a spirituality which has ceased to struggle and which therefore has ceased to be in Christ. So as our culture spawns numerous privatised spiritualities, thousands die of the cold.

To recognise in the pain of others, in the broken and crushed people of the world, the form of the wounded Christ, is to recognise the strange and demanding nature of the gospel call. It is the call to perform the corporal works of mercy: to feed the hungry; to clothe

the naked; to shelter the homeless poor; to break the
fetters of injustice; to give drink to the thirsty; to visit
the sick; to bury the dead. It is a call to gird ourselves
with Christ's dirty towel and to wash his feet, those
bloody, wounded, exhausted feet. Christ's feet, his
wounded hands and side, his broken heart, are not to
be found only in ancient Jerusalem, but in Manchester
and London, in Chicago and Boston, in Santiago and
Johannesburg, in the back streets of the earth, wherever
his sisters and brothers are crushed and broken and
cast down as persons of no significance.

THE SOCIAL CROSS

The social meaning of the passion has to be worked
out in blood and tears and anguish in each generation.
It has to be worked out in struggle and perplexity and
pain in every parish and in every Christian person. It
has to be worked out in London and other cities where
thousands share in the brokenness, the cruelty, the
violence inflicted upon Christ. Where is Christ's passion, and our response, in all this pain? It is not surprising that the devotion called the Stations of the Cross
has acquired a whole new significance in Latin America
where it is closely linked with the struggle for justice.
Indeed many simple acts of prayer and mercy acquire
new meaning in a cold climate. Within our present
climate of institutionalised cruelty and neglect, to perform the works of mercy is a virtually subversive
activity. It is to see our society from the underside,
from the perspective of its Bethlehems and its Calvaries.
It is to see the suffering of the most despised as the
suffering of God.

Christ as criminal, Christ as madman, Christ as alcoholic vagrant: all this and more is implied in the unconditional identification of God with the victim.[11]

All Christian service, all true theology, starts at the cross, starts where God suffers now, starts where the pain is. And we have no excuse for not recognising the face of Christ. As Sheila Cassidy reminds us:

> We know well enough what he looked like: like any desperate Kurd or Slav, stumbling barefoot over mountain paths, eyes blinded by tears, shoulders bowed with fatigue. He looked like the youngster I ignored yesterday in the street, a bedraggled booted teenager, sitting hopelessly on the pavement clutching a mongrel puppy, her face contorted with emptiness and pain. We know what he looked like: what we need to learn is how to comfort him suffering here and now.[12]

For this to happen, preaching and action must be closely linked. A Church which gathers to hear a sermon, and whose members then engage in 'social action', as it were, on the side, is in an unhealthy and dangerous state. Unless the proclamation (*kerygma*) and the service (*diakonia*) are in the closest possible relationship, trouble is inevitable. It is when our theology and our social commitment meet in prayer that we can genuinely say, with Thomas Traherne:

> O Christ, I see thy cross of thorns in every eye, thy bleeding naked wounded body in every soul, thy

death liveth in every memory. Thy crucified person is embalmed in every affliction, thy pierced feet are bathed in everyone's tears, and it is my privilege to enter with thee into every soul.

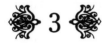

A Kingdom
not of This World

My kingdom is not from this world.   (John 18:36)

JESUS IN CONTEXT

We cannot expect to make sense of the death of Jesus without an attempt to understand his life and background. He was born into a double system of exploitation in Palestine. While the Roman empire imposed economic control through taxes and political control through its officials, the Palestinian state operated through the Temple which demanded economic contributions in the form of tithes and other funds.

Jesus came from the most troublesome of all the Jewish districts, Galilee, with its unique social and political character. The word means district (*gelil*) and was used specifically of the district beyond the River Jordan ('Galilee of the nations', Isaiah 9:1), but it was far more than a geographical description. The term 'Galilee' was associated in popular consciousness with Judas the Galilean and with other leaders of insurrections. From Galilee arose all the revolutionary move-

ments which disturbed the Romans. It was the scene
of guerrilla warfare and of nationalist uprisings. The
years from AD 30 to 70 were seething with revolts. To
be a Galilean at all was to be suspect. Pilate had mixed
the blood of Galilean rebels with sacrifices (Luke 13:1).
Yet we are constantly misled by hymns which speak of
'Sabbath rest by Galilee [and] calm of hills above' when
in fact Galilee meant trouble. As a child, Jesus would
have witnessed the destruction of the town of Sepph-
oris, a few miles from Nazareth, and the annihilation
of its population.

This was the geographical context of Jesus' birth. He
was born in the specific circumstances of a census
which had been set up in order to implement the poll
tax. Ninety per cent of the population of Galilee were
peasants. These oppressed peasants were 'the people'
who, according to the gospels, heard Jesus gladly. The
burden of taxation was the central economic fact of life,
and led to class conflict with the priestly aristocracies,
so much so that in AD 66 rebels burnt the record of
debts in the Temple. There was high unemployment,
with many looking for work, and the violence went far
beyond Herod's slaughter of the innocent children.

It was out of this deeply disturbed climate of alienation, upheaval and resistance that the 'marginal Jew'[1]
called Jesus came. This climate of colonial rule,
oppressive taxation, accumulating debt and bankruptcy,
forced migration and revolutionary uprisings, formed
the background to Jesus' proclamation of the Kingdom
of God (Mark 1:14).

So Jesus had a context, a base. In fact he had several
bases. His geographical base was Galilee and the resistance movements against the Roman oppressors. His

religious, or ideological, base was that of progressive Pharisaism, respectable religion, the movement for a holy nation, not all that different from the Church of England at its best. He was called rabbi. He recalled his hearers to the 'weightier matters of the law'. It was this group which he challenged most fiercely and repudiated most totally, probably because he realised that his followers throughout the ages were most likely to revert to Pharisaism – as indeed they have done and continue to do. It was for this liberal religious culture that Jesus reserved his fiercest and most uncompromising language.

Against this he set his personal base, the apostles and the band of faithful women, the culture of the dispossessed whom he trained, radicalised and endowed with the power of the age to come. And that power was not seen merely as a future prospect but as an active present force. Salvation meant bread and forgiveness from debt.

So, gathering around him a rabble of fishermen, Zealot sympathisers and various riff-raff, he moved through this troubled region, teaching, healing, setting people free. The early chapters of Mark's Gospel show him healing, exorcising, cleansing lepers, and forgiving sins. He ate with sinners and tax collectors, and broke the Sabbath, claiming that the Son of Man was Lord of the Sabbath. The common people heard him gladly. The religious authorities saw him as a serious threat and, as a result of his activities, conspired to destroy him (Mark 3:6). The Romans saw him as subverting the lawful rule of Caesar. The picture that we find is not of a 'gentle Jesus meek and mild' but more like that given by Conrad Noel when he described Jesus

as 'a rebel born in the shed of a public house, who
called his king a silly jackal, who broke the conventions
of society, who defied the world, broke the law, was
hunted by the police, and was destroyed by the coalition
of the worldlings and the next worldlings'.[2]

THE RECOVERY OF KINGDOM THEOLOGY
AND KINGDOM VISION

We are in danger of missing all this because the form
of the gospel that we have inherited in the west has
been diluted, individualised and interiorised. Two texts
have been used in support of this process of reducing
the range and impact of the gospel. One is the phrase
'The Kingdom of God is within you' (Luke 17:21, King
James Version). It is argued, or rather assumed without
argument, that Jesus taught a belief in a kingdom
within the heart of the believer, an entirely interior
experience, perhaps of warmth and peace. It is
extremely unlikely that *entos humon* could mean
'within you', and it is normally translated as 'amongst
you' or 'in the midst of you'. In any case, 'you' is plural,
so even 'within' would refer to the presence of the
Kingdom within a community. An interior understanding makes nonsense of the gospels and shows the
influence of post-sixteenth-century western ideas. The
notion of an interior 'spiritual' kingdom would have
been wholly without meaning to the people of Jesus'
time.

The other text is from John, where Jesus apparently
claimed that his Kingdom was 'not of this world' (John
18:36). The phrase 'this world' was unusual and
uniquely Christian. It is not found in classical writers

or in the Old Testament. Here there is only one world, including heaven and earth, but not two worlds. But as used in John and Paul, the term refers to two ages, two realms. The Kingdom of God stands in contrast to, and in conflict with, the structures and values of this age. When Jesus says that his Kingdom is not of (or, more accurately, from) this world, he does not mean that it has nothing to do with this world, but that its origins and values originate elsewhere, that it stands over and against this world (or age) as a symbol of judgement upon it.

In fact the good news of the Kingdom of God is revolutionary news. The Kingdom is 'otherworldly' in the strict sense that it operates as a critical process within human history, a constant symbol of the other world, a sign of transcendence. It is a source of change and transformation for this world, a vision and impulse for a new world. For many years this message has been evaded and its impact ignored. In 1923 Percy Widdrington, a prophetic figure in the Church of England, said that the recovery of the Kingdom of God as a hope for the transformation of this world and as 'the regulative principle of theology' would bring about a reformation in the Church compared with which the sixteenth-century reformation would seem a small event. Today we are witnessing part of the fulfilment of which he spoke. One of the most encouraging features of recent Christian history has been the recovery of this sense of the conflictual and world-transforming dimension in Kingdom theology and vision. For too long the Church has evacuated the good news of the Kingdom of God of all its dynamic content. Now we are seeing a recovery of the biblical message that the

Kingdom will transform the structures of this world and will stand for ever. Once this has been recovered, simplistic divisions between religion and politics collapse.

A turning point for many evangelical Christians was the Lausanne Conference on World Evangelisation in 1974. At this gathering Billy Graham, a well-known 'evangelist' and close ally of the Nixon regime (and of earlier presidents) in the USA, claimed that social justice was 'not our primary concern'. The rejection of his dualistic theology, in which evangelism and justice were separated, marked a crisis in evangelical thought and a moment of renewal. It was part of a process of recovery of biblical wholeness which had been going on for some time. Two years earlier John Howard Yoder had published his important study *The Politics of Jesus*, in which he argued both that the message of Jesus offered a revolutionary political vision, and also that the Church, the community of the followers of Jesus, was the primary social structure in which the gospel was to be manifested. Soon afterwards Richard Mouw, another leading American evangelical, claimed that political activity was an integral part of evangelism. The phrase 'radical discipleship' entered the vocabulary of Christians. And soon Jim Wallis, who, as the key figure in the Sojourners community in Washington DC, had played a major role in the recovery of biblical radicalism, was pointing out that the gospel as preached in most conventional western settings had been moulded to suit a narcissistic culture. It sought to bring Jesus into our lives instead of bringing us into his. The gospel as preached in the west no longer helped to turn the world upside down but rather served to reinforce its false values and structures. This was to a large extent because the content of the message had changed. Indeed, Wallis argued, the gospel as preached in most churches 'bears almost no resemblance to the original evangel'. Evangelism, as a call to a new way of life, should lead to the spread of social deviance and undermine the economic and political system; the impact of the conventional message was rather to reinforce conventional life-styles.[3]

Recently we have seen the 'Kingdom Manifesto on the Whole Gospel' which has emerged from a conference of evangelical, charismatic and pentecostal movements held in Malaysia in March 1994. The overall impact of this movement has been that many Christians have come to see that the gospel of Jesus Christ cannot be divorced from politics. An apolitical Jesus has no meaning. Such a view cannot cope with his life and ministry, with his teaching, with the cross, the death reserved for political agitators and threats to the *status quo*, or with the radical life-style of the Early Church.

JESUS: TAX, FOOD AND TEMPLE

Jesus' death was not an isolated act: it was the inevitable conclusion of his life. It is clear from the gospel records that Jesus was a divisive figure. As Simeon had predicted, he divided many hearts. His life and ministry were filled with controversy, and we can discern a threefold conflict – with the quietism of the pietists, with the Sadducean establishment, and with the violence of the Zealots. In the course of his life, three issues were of critical importance – tax, food and the Temple.

The question of taxation was one of the hottest issues

of the time. In addition to the ordinary Roman tax, the Temple had received special permission from Rome to collect its own tax (Matthew 17:24–26). A question was asked about whether it was lawful to pay taxes to the emperor (Caesar) or not (Mark 12:13–17). Jesus' reply was to ask whose was the inscription on the coin, and, when told that it was the emperor's, he replied, 'Give to the emperor the things that are the emperor's, and to God the things that are God's'. The synoptic writers tell us that the people were 'amazed' by his answer.

They would certainly have been amazed at the way in which this answer has been used in recent polemic by those who wish to assert the apolitical character of Jesus' ministry and to exalt the claims of the secular power. So the British politician Enoch Powell has claimed that 'he was denying in the most precise manner the relevance of his mission to politics and economics', while Margaret Thatcher assured us that 'Jesus got it about right' in his statement.[4] Both seem to assume not only that Jesus was carefully (and conveniently) avoiding the realm of political controversy but also that he was accepting and promoting a view of the world in which the two realms, Caesar's and God's, were carefully separated. Caesar's realm, on this view, represents that of politics and public affairs, while God's realm is reserved for 'spiritual' matters. But this is to misunderstand and distort both text and context, and it makes nonsense of the whole of Jewish history and theology and of Jesus' own teaching. In fact he undermined the whole question about taxation by asserting the absolute claim of God. Jesus did not claim that God and Caesar controlled autonomous or equally important realms, but that God's claim was absolute

and Caesar's was relative. In doing so he cut at the very
root of the imperial claims to domination, as the people
realised for they were apparently pleased with his reply
– a fact which is inexplicable on the conventional view.
In fact, at his trial before Pilate the issue of tax was
still being raised as one of the accusations of sedition
against him (Luke 23:2).

A second area in which the subversive character of
Jesus' life is brought out is in his practice of eating
meals with all kinds of people, breaking both social and
ritual codes in doing so. It is important to notice how
central this practice of eating is in the ministry of
Jesus. There is no chapter of Luke's Gospel in which
food is not mentioned, and the sharing of a common
meal figures prominently in the gospel accounts. It
was these shared meals, these visible parables of the
Kingdom, which, with the Passover celebration, formed
the basis of later Christian eucharistic worship.

But what is significant is the kind of people whom
he invited – the sinners, the outcasts, the tax collectors
and publicans, disreputable types, as well as the ritually
unclean, the maimed, the crippled and the blind. Such
people were specifically excluded from sharing the holy
bread. Leviticus 21 lists them: the blind, the mutilated,
the handicapped. It is these people whom Jesus invites.
The religious authorities saw such behaviour as sacri-
legious: to the political powers it was seditious. In a
sense we can say that Jesus was killed because of the
way he ate and the company he kept.

What was Jesus doing in this practice of eating with
outcasts and rejects? He was asserting, in the most
open and dramatic way, that in the Kingdom of God
there were no outcasts or rejects, and that by virtue of

this, the Kingdom was bound to come into fatal colli-
sion with those who defended divisions of class, caste
and hierarchy. Linked with this was his fundamental
questioning of accepted kinship patterns, insisting that
his family consisted of those who did the will of God
(Mark 3:35).

But it was his attack on the Temple, the centre of
financial operations, which was the major factor in the
build-up to the crucifixion. It could be argued that
the accounts of Jesus' time in Jerusalem are among the
most political sections in the whole of the Bible. His
life was a threat to the sacred and to the *status quo*, to
religious purity and political order. He chose the most
visible symbol of complicity between the occupying
power and the religious authorities. For the Temple
represented the intersection of the Roman money
market and the local economy. Here he seems to have
performed a material exorcism, an act of cleansing,
using words from two prophets, Isaiah and Jeremiah.
(Jeremiah, soon after he had uttered those words, was
imprisoned.) During the polemic prior to his trial, the
words 'Destroy this temple and in three days I will raise
it up' were important. The cleansing scene seems to
have been viewed as a messianic claim, for the prophet
Malachi had predicted that the Lord would suddenly
come to his Temple.

NON-POLITICAL JESUS?

It can only be seriously maintained that the ministry
of Jesus was 'non-political' by defining the concept of
the political in the narrowest possible way. It was a
subversive ministry, a *diakonia* or servanthood, which

involved the undermining of fixed roles and their reversal. The washing of feet, which in John's Gospel replaces the eucharistic institution, symbolises that servanthood. It is depressing to reflect that had Christian worship been centred on feet washing rather than bread breaking, today we would be embroiled in debates about whether immersion was necessary or whether sprinkling would suffice; whether the left foot should be washed before the right; whether women's feet could be washed at all; and whether women could wash feet. But the political significance of the feet washing lies in its total subversion and reversal of hierarchy: for it is the master who washes the feet of the disciples, the first becomes last, the last first. As Mary prophesied, the mighty are put down and the humble are uplifted. For this is an upside-down kingdom in which conventional values and structures are overturned. The feet washing stands as a permanent symbol of Christian ministry. Christ whose form is divine assumes the form of a slave and calls his followers to the practice of the same subversive humility.

Yet our gentrified and privatised reading of the gospels misses all this and produces a gentle, apolitical, non-threatening, liberal Jesus, a Jesus divested of all his revolutionary significance. Such a distortion makes the cross inexplicable. Jesus is torn from his context and all that remains of him is his name.

One of the most widespread and persistent images of Jesus is that of the great reconciler, one who promotes tolerance and harmony wherever he goes. Non-Christians often pay respect to 'the spirit of Jesus' as a spirit of goodwill, tolerance and kindness. This is to ignore a great deal in the accounts which suggest that, far from producing harmony, Jesus produced division, bringing not peace but a sword, setting members of families against one another, and leading to anger and social unrest. Yet we too easily emphasise reconciliation without seeing these other aspects. In one study in the Methodist Church, 42 per cent of ministers said that reconciliation was the first task of the Church. But what does this mean? Certainly there is no idea in the New Testament of reconciliation with the powers of darkness, hence the centrality of the exorcisms in Jesus' ministry. Evil forces are to be cast out, not reconciled. Reconciliation is the result of the struggle, and is brought about only through conflict and eventually through death itself.

THE POLITICAL MEANING
OF THE CROSS

So Jesus died the death reserved for rebels and criminals, threats to the stable order: death by crucifixion. Josephus described many crucifixions outside Jerusalem, all of them for rebellion. Crucifixion was particularly used to subjugate people, and often its victims were slaves. When the rebellion of Spartacus failed, six hundred rebellious slaves were crucified on the Appian Way. Jesus was crucified between two criminals. The whole affair – arrest, trial and death – has the atmosphere of an intensely political drama, with conspiracy, deals, torture, covert action, arguments about exchanges of prisoners, plans for manipulation of the authorities, and finally the judicial killing.

Yet out of this death emerges a new community, born from the experience of the cross, the ultimate challenge to worldly power. Early Christian writers describe the achievement on the cross in political terms, as a despoiling of the principalities and powers. It is only from that tree of shame that Jesus claims to be Lord. But to assert 'Jesus is Lord' is to deny all earthly claims to absolute authority. If Jesus is Lord, there is no other. So the community identified with the cross becomes marginal to the power structures, disobedient to their false claims, aliens and sojourners, its only home being outside the gate. The stable order is undermined. The early writer Celsus complained that the Christians had introduced *stasis*, revolution, into both heaven and earth. Caesar had done his worst.

Throughout history the cross stands as a symbol of protest and of revolt: protest against all claims, whether by religious or political power, to absolute unquestioning control over human minds and bodies; revolt against all systems and ideologies, all regimes and institutions, which continue to push individuals and groups beyond the pale, outside the gate. The cross stands as a symbol of the falsehood and demonic nature of all religions which sanctify established injustice, religions of the *status quo*, which continue to reproduce Calvaries all over the world. The cross is a crisis point for all societies which seek to produce men and women of quiescence, men and women who are trained to give unquestioning, uncritical obedience to worldly powers and not to Christ; a crisis point for all systems of violence, systems which are bound to lead to the reproduction of Calvaries great and small; a crisis point for all who despise the weak and small people, and in so doing despise Christ.

Against all temptations to conformity and compromise stands the politics of Jesus who nailed the false claims to lordship to his cross, and by doing so created a liberated zone, a climate in which Christian resistance can grow even in dark ages like ours. So today, as yesterday, Christ stands against the powers, against the oppressive structures which maintain injustice and cruelty, denying life and wholeness to many. The crucified Christ hangs outside the gate of the city. Condemned and judged, he himself is judge of all.

It is the claim of the Christian community that through the cross we have been delivered from the present evil age and from 'the elemental spirits of the world to which we were enslaved' (Galatians 1:4; 4:3). Through the cross Christ has disarmed the powers, the rulers and authorities, and triumphed over them (Colossians 2:15). Yet the struggle continues and, in Christ, we are still engaged in a warfare with principalities and powers, the rulers of this present dark age (Ephesians 6:12). This warfare is central to the task of Christian discipleship today.

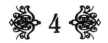

The Love of God
Poured Out

*God's love has been poured into our hearts through
the Holy Spirit that has been given to us.*

(Romans 5:5)

THE DISCIPLINE OF DISCIPLESHIP

Christianity goes disastrously and dangerously wrong
when Jesus is worshipped but not followed. We call
out 'Lord, Lord' but do not follow what he said. His
name appears on the banners and stamps and placards,
but it might as well be Elvis Presley or Donald Duck
or Superman – or, for that matter, Hitler, Mussolini or
Gadhafi. No notice is taken of his teaching or his
demands. There is a devotion, a loyalty of a kind, but
it is not to Jesus the person who lived, taught, healed,
died and rose. It is to Jesus as a mascot, a talisman, a
cultic idol. When this kind of distortion takes place,
nothing remains of Jesus but his name, or maybe his
image. The crucifix is divested of its power and meaning
and instead becomes an object of superstitious addic-
tion. The death of Jesus is torn out of the historical

and prophetic context of his life and work. The power of the cross, what Luther called the 'left handed power of God', is evacuated of content as well as context.

What I mean is that the preaching of the cross itself can go awry. Preaching can become cut off from life, from community, from any kind of social and political structures in which the cross could become active and effective. So the cross is proclaimed only within a sanitised zone and within a charmed world of rhetoric and mannerism. The language becomes increasingly sentimental, cut off from any concrete reality. The words and symbols spill over us but have no impact. We have lost the crucial dimension of discipleship, of following in 'the way of the cross'.

To follow the way of the cross is to enter into a relationship of tremendous power and strength of action. The early Christians were recognised as those who had turned the world upside-down (Acts 17:6), a recognition of the dynamic in the preaching and the corporate life which arose from it. At the heart of this preaching and life was the memory and the life of the crucified one. But the Jesus who died, the Jesus who was deliberately killed, was the same Jesus who taught, who went about doing good (Acts 10:37ff.), who healed the sick, cleansed the lepers, and cast out the forces of evil. It was the Jesus who, in his first appearance in the Nazareth synagogue, made his mission and his strategy perfectly plain.

> The Spirit of the Lord is upon me
> because he has anointed me to bring good news
> to the poor.

> He has sent me to proclaim release to the
>   captives
> and recovery of sight to the blind,
> to let the oppressed go free,
> to proclaim the year of the Lord's favour.
>
> (Luke 4:18–19)

To take this sermon seriously is to realise the mistake of separating evangelism from justice, spirituality from social action, prayer from politics. It should also lead us to see that the community of disciples of Jesus is called to adopt the same priorities of proclamation, healing and liberation which are outlined in his own manifesto.

A JUBILEE PEOPLE

In other words, we are called to be a Jubilee people, for it is the Year of Jubilee which is the central motif of this passage, taken from Isaiah 61. The theme of 'release', encompassing both the land and individuals, has its origins in Leviticus 25, the proclamation of liberty in the Jubilee Year. The theme is taken up again in Isaiah 61, a further proclamation of liberty, in which 'prisoners' probably refers to those who are the victims of poverty and economic oppression. However, in his use of the passage, Jesus inserts the phrase 'to let the oppressed go free' from Isaiah 58:6, a way of emphasising even more strongly that it is deliverance from oppression which is his central concern. So the Year of Jubilee, the year of freedom, of release for captives, and deliverance from debt, and of restoration of the land to the people, was the symbolic framework of his message.

He comes to proclaim the year of God's favour, the Year of Jubilee.

We saw in the last chapter that debt was a major problem in Galilee because of Herod's oppressive taxes, and the theme of debt is a recurring one in Jesus' teaching. Over and over again, the teachings and the parables focus on debt: it is the paradigm of social evil, the context of Jesus' message of release, of liberation. The Year of Jubilee, when debts were cancelled, is an ideal symbol for his proclamation.

But the core of the Jubilee theme is that of land. If the symbol of liberation in the Mosaic tradition is the Exodus, the symbol of equality within the liberated territory is that of the Year of Jubilee. The principle of the Jubilee is that of equitable distribution of the land between the tribes (Leviticus 25), and as such it was the cornerstone of Israel's ethical practice. Behind it lies the fundamental principle that the land belongs to God. It is part of the redemptive process, part of the covenant. There is no absolute right of ownership of land. George Dalmon put it well in a hymn written for Thaxted Church in Essex:

> God is the only landlord
> To whom our rents are due.
> God made the earth for everyone
> And not for just a few.
> The four parts of creation,
> Earth, water, air and fire,
> God made and ranked and stationed
> For everyone's desire.

Jesus came to fulfil the law and the prophets, and a

major aspect of his teaching was his emphasis on 'the weightier matters of the law, justice and mercy and faith' (Matthew 23:23). A community which is faithful to this teaching will place the liberation of the earth and its oppressed and captive peoples at the centre of its understanding and discipleship.

So the good news proclaimed by Jesus was about liberation, and this good news was to be embodied in a new community, the Kingdom of God, a new age of new relationships. It was good news of transformation, of reversal of fortunes, a message not about a private salvation of soul, but about corporate righteousness. To be a Christian is to be part of this new community – a community which is committed to the pursuit of righteousness.

The idea of a community committed to righteousness is linked to the Jewish theme of covenant. The whole of Jewish history is based on the belief that God has entered into a two-way relationship with individuals and with a community. Old Testament history revolves around the structural relationships involved in being a covenant people and the betrayals, infidelities and ups and downs of this relationship. As the history progresses, the covenant is seen as interior as well as exterior (Jeremiah 31) and there is a link between the covenant and ecological peace (Ezekiel 34). This theme is taken up by Paul in Romans 8 when he places the glorious liberty of the children of God within the wider framework of the groaning of the creation as it awaits its deliverance from slavery and oppression. Salvation is corporate and cosmic. It is to this corporate and cosmic character of salvation that the symbol 'Kingdom of God' bears witness.

A KINGDOM PEOPLE

If there is one fact about which New Testament scholars are agreed, it is that 'the good news of the Kingdom of God' was the heart of Jesus' preaching. Take away the references to the Kingdom in the gospels, and there is no gospel at all. Yet it is common to hear what passes for Christianity preached without reference to the Kingdom of God.

The Kingdom of God was a phrase with a history. It was the heart of the prophetic hope for a new age of justice and mercy when the earth would be filled with the glory of God and when all common things would be holy. It is a deeply Jewish hope, rooted in a Jewish understanding of God in history. Outside of this Jewish approach to history and the world, Jesus makes no kind of sense: this is why the anti-semitic strand in Christianity which blames the Jewish people for his death is so dangerously mistaken. More than any other figure Jesus vindicates and affirms the Jewish religious vision – the vision of spirit embodied and manifested within a community of men and women who seek justice and holiness together, and who realise that it is only within such a community of commitment that justice and holiness can ever be found.

Jesus' hearers would have had no doubt about the serious consequences of his message. His critics and opponents would have been bothered, not about what he meant, but about the possibility that it might happen. His followers – the poor, the outcasts, the common folk, the women – knew what he was on about, rejoiced at his words, but did not reckon with the fact that there was no way to the Kingdom which did not pass through the cross.

The cross and the Kingdom are intimately connected because the Kingdom of God can never come by gentle progress. Only by tribulation and crisis can the new world emerge from the ruins of the old. The cross stands as a perpetual symbol of the truth that the world system is organised against the Kingdom of God, and that religious powers are just as likely to resist its demands as are political ones. (Indeed throughout much of human history they are the same people!) The gospel is concerned with judgement and crisis because it was born in judgement and crisis. It was for judgement that Jesus came into the world. The gospel is itself a crisis, a dislocation of order. The language of the tradition is filled with words for change – the proclamation of the Day of the Lord, the descent of the New Jerusalem from heaven to earth, the call to repentance, to a total renewal of life. Redemption is a process which takes place within the framework of distress and chaos, the collapse of institutions and power structures, the disruption of earth and seas, the shaking of the powers of heaven, with people's hearts failing them for fear. It is when such things occur that we are to lift up our heads because our liberation is near. It is against such a background of upheaval that we are called to 'bear the cross'.

The demands of the Kingdom of God are extreme and absolute. Those who look back, those who make reservations, whose family and personal commitments take precedence, cannot follow the narrow way. The proclamation of the Kingdom of God by Jesus is a proclamation of the most extreme and risky type. It involves what Jesus calls taking up our own cross and even losing our own lives for the sake of the cause.

> If any want to become my followers, let them deny themselves and take up their cross and follow me. For those who want to save their life will lose it, and those who lose their life for my sake, and for the sake of the gospel, will save it. (Mark 8:34–35).

Like many of the 'hard sayings' of Jesus, this sounds impossible. It is only possible through the power of the cross itself by which we have in fact been crucified. This is what Paul means when he speaks of the destruction of the old self.

> We know that our old self was crucified with him so that the body of sin might be destroyed, and we might no longer be enslaved to sin ... But if we have died with Christ, we believe that we will also live with him. (Romans 6:6–8)

It is only through solidarity in the cross that we can attain solidarity and communion with God in the life of the new age. There is no short cut.

What does it mean to bear the cross? The phrase, as it occurs in the passage from Mark 8:34 quoted above, may refer to the practice of actually marking people with the cross. This ancient practice of marking people on the forehead was well known. The prophet Ezekiel put a mark on the foreheads of those who groaned and sighed for the abominations committed in Jerusalem before the slaughter of the idolaters

(Ezekiel 9:4), while in Revelation 7:3 the servants of God were sealed on their foreheads before the day of destruction. To be a Christian is to be signed with the mark of the cross, the baptismal mark of incorporation into Christ. To bear the cross in solidarity with Jesus is not to endure some mysterious kind of suffering which is thrust upon us, still less is it a way of describing an interior psychological attitude or orientation. It is a path freely chosen, the social reality of committing oneself in this world to the values of the world to come. This is clearly a call to lose one's life for the sake of the gospel. It is not a call to imitate Jesus as a figure from the past but to follow the risen and present Jesus of today. Christians do not maintain the memory of a dead Jesus: grieving over the body was prevented by the very large stone which was rolled away from the tomb before the grief could get under way (Mark 16:4). To respond to the cross is to follow, to share; it is to be a disciple. It is to respond to a new and amazing relationship of co-operation with God which is utterly different from the relationship of slave to master. We are sealed not as slaves but as children, as inheritors of the Kingdom of God.

THE SERVANT MESSIAH

I want now to look at three aspects of the following of Jesus: those of servanthood (*diakonia*), of non-violence and of love (including love of enemies). Jesus becomes a servant and calls us to a servant ministry in this new order in which conventional relationships are subverted. There are two words for servant in the New Testament – *diakonos* and *doulos*. *Diakonos* refers to one who serves or ministers and is one of a number of 'service' words from which we get our words 'deacon' and 'diaconate'. *Doulos,* on the other hand, refers to the condition of slavery, of being owned by another. Jesus tells his followers that whoever would be important must become a *doulos* because the Son of Man came not to be served but to serve (*diakonein*) (Mark 10:44–45).

During the late 1950s and the 1960s there was considerable debate in Church circles about the meaning and implications of these servant concepts. In fact there were four debates going on. There was a debate among New Testament scholars about the influence of Isaiah 52 and 53, the 'suffering servant' passages, on the treatment of the suffering of Jesus in the gospels, a debate which reached an important stage with the publication of Morna Hooker's major study *Jesus and the Servant* (1959). Running alongside this debate was a second one about the meaning of 'Son of Man' and 'Kingdom of God' in the gospels. What does 'Son of Man' mean? Does it originate in Ezekiel, Daniel or Enoch, or all three? Does it reflect lowliness or glory? Is it individual or corporate? And what is the 'service' to which the Son of Man is called? Then there was a debate, apparently running along quite different lines, about sacrifice and priesthood. Theologians such as Eugene Masure, Eric Mascall and Max Thurian were questioning medieval notions of sacrifice, while the Second Vatican Council seemed to be putting forward a new understanding both of the eucharist and of Christian ministry. One of the results of this was the re-emergence of the permanent diaconate. Finally, there was the debate about the 'servant church' associated with the World

Council of Churches and in England with clergy in the Diocese of Southwark. In all these debates the notion of *diakonia*, servanthood or ministry, occupied a key place.[1]

While apparently unconnected, these debates raised related issues – about who Jesus was, what he did, and how it affects his followers. They opened up complex areas of thought about sacrifice and ministry. Whatever areas of disagreement remain, it seems clear that Jesus calls his disciples to follow him in the way of lowly servanthood, and that this is linked with his vocation as a suffering Son of Man. This suffering is redemptive, sacrificial, and to share in his sacrifice is to share Christ's priesthood. Priesthood in fact is at heart a sharing in the dying and rising of Christ, a priesthood in which the whole body of Christ, not just ordained ministers, is involved. We are baptised into servanthood and into solidarity, into *diakonia* and into priesthood. We are baptised for service to the world. So in the American Book of Common Prayer the candidate for baptism is asked: 'Will you seek and serve Christ in all persons . . . ?' and is later welcomed to 'share . . . in his eternal priesthood'. There will be no renewal of the meaning of the cross in the Christian life unless there is a renewal of the liturgy and meaning of baptism.

THE NON-VIOLENT CROSS

The New Testament is a unique record of the emergence of an ethic of non-violence, distinct from the 'holy war' tradition. This ethic is quite out of character with the mainstream messianic expectation which was linked with violence and eventually led to the Jewish

War. In contrast to the collaborationist policies of the Sadducees, the liberal reformism of the Pharisees and the insurrectionary violence of the Zealots, Jesus offers a different model, that of suffering servant who undermines the foundations of the violent order.

The followers of Jesus are taught not to fight the demons with their own weapons. To do so merely demolishes the demonic structures while the demons transfer to one's own address: fighting with demons by their own methods is the best way to become demonic. So Jesus consistently rejects the way of violence, teaching his disciples not to resist evil (Matthew 5:39). It has been pointed out that all the conditions for a just war were in place at Gethsemane – a just cause, self-defence, the tactic of last resort, and a good chance of success. But they were rejected. And undoubtedly the early Christians took this rejection as binding upon them and as an intrinsic part of their discipleship. From the end of the New Testament period until AD 170–180 there is no evidence of Christians in the army, while as late as the early third century, the Canons of Hippolytus ruled that soldiers must be taught not to kill and to refuse to do so if commanded.

The rejection of this teaching ultimately leads to some kind of fascism, rooted as it is in the cult of violence. The cross becomes twisted into a swastika, or into a weapon with which to crush one's opponents. In the fascist vision, which is the antithesis of the Christian vision, violence is an instrument of purification and brings out the best in us. And there is no doubt that the cult of violence can and does inspire heroism and leads people to take risks for the sake of what is seen as a worthy cause. Yet ultimately it destroys its own followers. The idea that violence can purify and cleanse us is a lie. Sadly many revolutionary movements, often composed of people too young to remember the era of fascism, have been seduced into believing this lie. So have many Christians, alarmed by the harsh demands of the call to non-violence.

Christians have never found this road of non-violent love easy. In fact the relationship of non-violence to truth and justice is extremely delicate. Passion and violence of heart can harm it, and once the violence ceases to disturb us, the harm done can be fatal. Our inner violence is particularly lethal when it is at its most 'spiritual' and least emotional. For if the violence acts in the depth of the will with no surface upheaval, the danger to the soul is very great indeed. Jesus perhaps saw that, at the end of the day, violence is always reactionary, because it treats people as objects. So those who are called to be peacemakers (and not simply peaceful people) need a spirituality of peace.

This must be a spirituality which recognises the tremendous obstacles in the path of non-violent discipleship. We ignore these at our peril. In A. S. Byatt's novel *The Game*, there is an account of a father who sacrificed his family to his spirituality, refusing to face the reality of evil and the depth of hostility to his values. One of his daughters comments:

> You always talk as though passive resistance could convert violence to love. But it can't and it doesn't and we ought to admit it. There will *always* be people who will slash open the other cheek when it is turned to them. In this life love will *not* overcome, it *will* not, it will go to waste and it is no

good to preach anything else. We need God because we are desperate and wicked and we can find him only through himself. The inner light doesn't necessarily shine and doesn't illuminate much. You will find no *meaning* by simply examining your consciences, maybe, ever. What I am saying is, we have got to find a way of *living* in a world that eats and destroys and pays nothing back.[2]

The way of the cross is a very hard way, and we should not embark upon it without counting the cost. Part of the preaching of the cross is the spiritual preparation of Christians for this path of non-violent love.

A COMMUNITY OF LOVE

The community which Jesus gathered together was to be a community characterised by mutual love. In this way people would know that they were his disciples. Love is described in the First Letter of John as the authentic proof of the resurrection. But the command to love goes beyond the community to embrace the love of enemies (Matthew 5:38–48; Luke 6:27–36). Enemies, *echthroi*, means both personal enemies and the enemies of the nation. It is this command rather than the command of love as such which is really unique about Jesus' teaching and goes beyond any comparable teaching in the tradition. (The command in Leviticus 19:17–18 was interpreted to mean loving one's fellow Israelites, not one's enemies, while the Qumran Manual of Discipline ordered members to hate the children of darkness.) The New Testament forbids hatred and insists that Christians are not instruments of God's vengeance. Indeed Tertullian (probably wrongly) claimed that Christians were the only people who loved their enemies. Certainly they were the only community who were commanded to do so.

Why does all this matter? It matters because the teaching about the Jubilee, the Kingdom, servanthood, non-violence and love is a teaching about the nature and character of God. In fact the term 'Kingdom of God' grew up as a kind of euphemism for God, a way of speaking about God without mentioning his name. To speak of God is to speak of a new community which lives according to justice and holiness: only within such a community can God be known and followed. God does not hover remotely, threateningly and antiseptically above the world: God is the ground of our belonging together, the source of our life together, the root of our humanity. As Julian of Norwich said, God is the ground in which we all stand.

So the Christian community, the Church, is an integral part of the good news. What we preach is what we are. The Early Church lived out the *koinonia* in terms of economic sharing (Acts 4:32–5:16; 2 Corinthians 8). The New Testament readings at Mass on the Fourth Sunday in Lent, over the three-year cycle, are about the character of the Christian community: a community called to be children of light (Ephesians 5:8–14), of love and risen life (Ephesians 2:4–10) and ministers of reconciliation within a new creation (2 Corinthians 5:17–21).

Jesus tells us that he is the vine and we the branches, one of the clearest expressions of solidarity. As the vine draws earth, water and air into itself, so Jesus draws us into his life. Christians, according to Ignatius of Antioch, are 'branches of the cross'. It was for such a revolutionary transformation of the whole idea of God that Jesus was killed. Yet what he was doing was taking the vision of the law and the prophets to its logical conclusion – that truth which was embodied in the Year of Jubilee: only when human beings struggle for freedom, for equality and for justice can the true God be known.

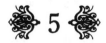

5

The Darkness where God Dwells

... the thick darkness where God was.

(Exodus 20:21)

... darkness came over the whole land....

(Matthew 27:45)

DARKNESS OVER ALL THE LAND

In one of her meditations Simone Weil made the disturbing comment that the distance between God and God can only be viewed from above. It is easier, she suggested, to see oneself as God the Creator than as the crucified God of Jesus. Weil sees the cross as marking the infinite distance between God and God. I suppose that part of what she meant was that it is only by setting a safe distance between ourselves and the terrible reality of the cross that we can begin to make sense of it without it threatening our sanity. Yet in order to speak of the crucified God we need a theology of abandonment, of dereliction, of an alienation so profound that it can only be expressed in language marked

by paradox and by great daring and risk. The crucifixion
of the Son of God by one of the most advanced civilis-
ations in the ancient world does not seem to be an
acceptable or reasonable method of redeeming the
world. There is something so outrageous and obscene
about it that the agony in Gethsemane becomes the
only comprehensible part of the whole saga. To admit
this is not faithlessness: it is to accept with brutal
honesty that none of us understands what this is all
about, and that we are drawn to it by a powerful and
inscrutable desire and love.

For surely it is this which hits us most powerfully
and which troubles and confuses us most when we
try to meditate on the cross: the utter desolation, the
brokenness, the darkness, the anguished and terrible
complexity of the scene. Christ hangs desolate, a solitary naked figure, suspended against the universe, the
only sign of the Kingdom that survives, the one symbol
of light amidst the prevailing night. It seems to be
tragic, cursed. In fact the act of crucifixion was cursed.
Anyone who hung on a tree was under God's curse
(Deuteronomy 21:23; Galatians 3:13.) In Greek tragedy
the curse is only destroyed when a pure victim suffers,
and, according to the early Christian writers, Jesus, the
pure Lamb of God, does bear our sins to the tree, does
become sin for us. It is a mystery too profound and too
deeply disturbing to be absorbed easily. So the encounter with the cross, whether in preaching, prayer or
personal struggle, is one which involves darkness and
a good deal of inner distress.

The cross is the ultimate darkness. And yet, according to the gospel testimony, that darkness is not tragic.
The gospels show Jesus not as a tragic figure, haunted

by fate, but as a faithful, trusting, though at times frightened, figure, who moves towards his death with courage, conviction and clarity. The shepherd lays down his life of his own free will. He enters the darkness in utter freedom and in full awareness of the outcome.

The Lamentations of Jeremiah are often read at the daily offices in Holy Week. They sing of loneliness and desolation, of bitter weeping in the night and of the absence of comfort, of exile and distress, of affliction and deep sorrow. 'Is it nothing to you, all you who pass by? Look and see if there is any sorrow like my sorrow...' (Lamentations 1:12). As Jesus approaches his death, there is distress and agitation (Mark 14:33), loud cries and tears in his agonised prayer in Gethsemane (Hebrews 5:7), the loud cry from the cross itself (Mark 15:37), the sense of forsakenness at the end (Mark 15:34; Psalm 22:2). There are two particularly explosive moments at the point of death: the loud cry and final *ruach* (breath or spirit) of Jesus, and the ripping of the Temple veil from top to bottom (Mark 15:38). Like that in Egypt before the Exodus (Exodus 10:21), the darkness at Calvary was a darkness that could be felt. But the 'loud cry' (Exodus 11:6) which accompanied the slaughter of the firstborn was replaced by the cry of Jesus in his desolation.

Simone Weil, however, goes beyond the outer darkness of the scene to the inner crisis which occurred in the death on the cross. She sees the cross as marking the infinite distance between God and God. The darkness of the cross is terrible because God is torn in two. The infinite distance between humanity and God is revealed as a distance within God. This is the deepest meaning of the cross. No one should ever attempt to play down the horror and desperate isolation of that night. To enter into it fully is to risk both faith and sanity. It is, in Kierkegaard's phrase, a 'night of the absolute'.

THE JOURNEY OF DARK FAITH

The Christian way, otherwise known as discipleship or the way of the cross, is marked by transitions from one level of being to another. The language which is used of it is language about journey, pilgrimage, exploration, and this is frequently accompanied by images of darkness and obscurity. The Old Testament readings at Mass on the Fifth Sunday in Lent relate to the pain and turmoil of transition from one stage to another. Ezekiel writes of the opening of graves (Ezekiel 37:12–14), Jeremiah of the new covenant (Jeremiah 31:31–34), and Second Isaiah of the waters in the wilderness (Isaiah 43:16–25). The gospel readings too speak of deliverance from death and sin. One of the gospel readings is the story of the raising of Lazarus. This Lazarus is often confused with the person of the same name who is described in Luke 16 as a symbol of eternal rest after great torment. The Lazarus who is such a central figure in John's Gospel, and whose story takes up almost the whole of Chapter 11, is unknown to the synoptic gospels. In John he is the beloved, the friend of Jesus ('Lord, he whom you love is ill': 11:3). So close is Jesus to Lazarus and his sisters that he was described as being 'deeply moved in spirit and troubled', or, in Raymond Brown's translation, he 'shuddered, moved with the deepest emotion'.

Movement, intensity of emotion, deep distress,

progress, ever-deepening obscurity, sudden change – this is the very stuff of the way of faith. And faith, according to St John of the Cross, is 'a certain and obscure habit of soul'.

As our journey of faith continues, we constantly encounter new threats, new challenges, and enter new stages of the journey, both individually and corporately. We entered new stages at Auschwitz and at Hiroshima, and somehow we need to absorb them into our understanding of the darkness of God. It may be, as Alan Ecclestone has suggested, that Auschwitz has to teach us what the crucifixion of Christ did not, that the experience of that enormous dark night of terror is the fire in which our religious life must be purged and reborn. Both Alan Ecclestone and Jim Garrison speak of the experience of God after Auschwitz and Hiroshima in very similar terms, both of them drawing on the imagery of darkness and of the night.[1]

Those who go to pieces in Holy Week – those for whom it is all too unbearable, too crazy, too threatening – those people have perhaps begun to enter in some strange way into the dreadful mystery of the passion. It cannot be seen or understood from the outside. Charles Raven once said of the experience of war: 'Those who can live in it may be purified: those who look on are usually defiled.' The cross is a sign of defilement for the onlooker: it is only a purifying and healing reality for those who share its terrible darkness. To know Christ and the power of his resurrection can only occur as a result of sharing his suffering and death, becoming like him in his death (Philippians 3:10). In fact, going to pieces is an essential part of the way of the cross. To enter into the mystery of Christ's dying is to experience what has been called 'positive disintegration', a breaking process, a spiritual void of turbulence and dereliction. It seems as if our whole being is disintegrating, but what are disintegrating are the defences which surround us. This is the beginning of liberation of our true being. So there is a necessary integration of the cross, a sharing in the dying of Jesus, so that it is no longer seen simply as an event external to us. In the words of John Donne's poem 'The Crosse':

> For when that Crosse ingrudg'd unto
>   you stickes
> Then are you to your selfe a Crucifixe.

It is essential to transcend the detached and unmoved devotion which makes of the cross a beautiful symbol but does not tremble and shake with fear at the horror and sheer unfathomable depth of it all. It is only in anguish and brokenness of spirit that we can begin and continue this journey. The only theology which can speak with effectiveness and meaning to people who have entered into the Good Friday experience is a theology which has itself encountered dread and despair, not just the sense of frustration and loss of hope about something, but that more fundamental existential despair of which Kierkegaard wrote. Only such a path can be truly called theology, for theology demands passion, anguish, doubt: if these are not present, there is no true engagement with the living God but only a fascination with or interest in the idea of god.

Those who have begun to understand something of the meaning of Good Friday seem to be composed of two groups, and maybe we all share something of each group's response. First, there are those for whom the truth is unbearable and who, because of this, move towards despair, perhaps towards suicide, as Simone Weil did. The darkness becomes overwhelming, the desolation futile, the future one without hope. So there is death, physical or interior, and a kind of descent into hell, but resurrection does not take place. Secondly, there are those who receive the word of the cross with relief, with joy, with exultation, and who see in this naked desolate figure the authentic symbol of their own liberation from the power of death.

The real tragedy of Good Friday was the death of Judas. This death was truly tragic, meaningless, violent and desperate. Much of my ministry has been spent with people who have died tragic deaths. Others have lived lives which have been devoid of hope. I think particularly of the experience of many heroin addicts as they moved towards despair. One young woman, now off heroin, wrote this meditation on Good Friday:

> As the clouds gathered together and prayed, draw-
> ing together their dark thundering brows to medi-
> tate upon the sweeping sickness of a generation and
> of thousands of bent, wailing walking sticks – aids
> for the physical and moulting: to the psychology
> books and green and honeydoped brown bottles, all
> drifting away on an endless sea . . . a wavering tide
> . . . On the words which hang in the air between
> the two of us: a dream that started somewhere
> under the black dripping longing listing pillars of
> mist, rotting away as everyone else has done to the
> strains of a whining careless love needle of Death

> ... The disciples lament from one death to a new
> Birth – and they've all gone now.

She went on to describe:

> the MAN weaned on wine, justified by junk, happy
> on hash, hung up on heroin, crucified by cocaine,
> and morbidly, on the telephone, to the mortuary
> with a final shot of morphine, to a gaunt ghastly
> grave from the rising soil.

Unless we can identify in some way with this loss of
hope, we have not begun to understand the Good Friday
experience. In fact only those who know something of
the meaning of despair can come to experience victory.
Only the dead can appreciate resurrection, and all
Christians must confront and experience the darkness
as they move along the way to death. One of the worst
aspects of the darkness which we face is the painful
fear that some of the darkness we encounter may not
be redeemable, that it may be the darkness of original
sin. Yet this too must be faced in trust and confidence.

This entry into the darkness is the very heart of faith
and of hope. To be a Christian at all is to enter this
dark night: the night in which we do not know the way
but in which God becomes luminously present. This
dark night is a paradigm of the paschal transformation
by which we are integrated into the life of God.

It was St John of the Cross in the sixteenth century
who first used the term 'dark night of the soul'. He is
often seen as a gloomy and morbid ascetic who has
helped to turn a joyful Christian life into one of gloom
and severity. But his teaching is that the darkness is

the light and the love, the ecstatic light of God as seen from our finite and fallen position. The darkness is the light. Only those who pass through the darkness can know the wonder of redeeming love and of the power of grace. The way of faith is obscure: as St John says, we travel by night.

If a central aim of the Christian life is to help people encounter and enter into the dark night of faith, then Christian worship needs to hold together lament and praise, grief and glory, the articulation of alienation from God and of desire for God. Much worship seems to be marked by a superficial cheerfulness which is deeply offensive to, and at the same time is of no help to, the person who is going through dark times. Authentic worship needs to avoid the one-dimensional temptation if it is to be true to the complexity of the human condition. It is a dialectic of crucifixion and resurrection – the lament of the self in its isolation and distance from God, and the canticle of praise in our joyful anticipation of the new life of the resurrection. The abandonment to God in the experience of the desolation of Calvary is an abandonment made in trust in the midst of apparent hopelessness; the abandonment in resurrection praise is marked by ecstasy and wonder at God's amazing grace. It is the fusion of lament and praise which inaugurates true communion. But it is important that Christians do not try to live constantly in 'Alleluia time' and ignore the darkness and 'the valley' which are still part of our experience in this world. The cry of pain, the public ritual processing of grieving, the ability to trust in one's pain and in others' pain within a solidarity of love: these are all necessary elements in a corporate spirituality. The

Desert Fathers rightly stress the need for inward grief (*penthos*) in the hearts of all Christian people.

PASTORAL CARE AND THE DARK NIGHT

Christ dies outside the gate of the city (Hebrews 13:12–13), dies as a marginal person. Ancient cities were often built in forest clearings and contained areas known as *limina*, marginal areas between the city walls and the beginnings of the forest. These liminal areas are decisive for pastoral work, they are twilight zones of the most crucial importance.

The parish in which I minister is called St Botolph without Aldgate. The 'without' is important, for the church stands 'without' the city gate. Just as it was 'without a city wall' that the Lord was crucified, so it is often immediately outside the gate, literal or meta-phorical, outside the frontiers of 'normal' society, that many people come to discover their identities, needs and futures. There is an experience here of a certain sense of lostness. It is here, on the margins, in the shadows, that priestly ministry is most urgently needed, but it will often be a ministry marked by silence, inter-cession, and solidarity in pain and desolation.

Priests are liminal people, living and operating on the margins between the city and the dark forest, between stability and madness, between the structures and the chaos. But the real home of the priest is outside the structures, for, like all Christians, she is an alien, a sojourner, a pilgrim. Priesthood is intimately bound up with darkness and with death, for 'it is the office which ritually, inwardly and ascetically shares the dying and rising of Christ'.[2] Ulrich Simon brings out the

importance of the priest within the horror of the con-
centration camp at Auschwitz, and in so doing he pene-
trates close to the heart of priestly identity.

> The priestly ideal uses and converts the nothingness
> which the world of Auschwitz offers. Here the
> priest's sacerdotal dedication encounters the
> vacuum with self-sacrifice ... The priest at the
> camp counts because he has no desires of self-
> importance and gives life because he stands already
> beyond extermination. He is the exact opposite to
> the king rat. The hour of darkness cannot take
> him by surprise since he has practised silence in
> darkness.[3]

More and more, as people experience new and frighten-
ing forms of darkness and despair, and as people are
thrust into the terrible priesthood of death through
HIV and AIDS, we need priestly ministry which has
understood and confronted this profound darkness of
Christ's dying and rising.

Much Christian pastoral activity, however, seems to
have as its aim the protection of people from any
encounter with this darkness. Religion is offered as a
place of refuge. Within the classical mystical tradition,
a major part of the work of spiritual direction consists
in helping people to move out of their false securities
to the point of disintegration and entry into the dark
night, and guiding them through the subsequent
upheaval and turmoil. Yet this is a far cry from the aim
and practice of conventional religion which offers a safe
neutrality in the face of chaos and horror. Much of
the religion which has flourished in recent years in the

'Christian' west is of this neutral type. It offers inner and often corporate security and warmth. It is a religion of comfort and reassurance. It offers no vision, no challenge, no striving towards the new.

I have suggested that in fact one of the central tasks of pastoral care is to help people enter the darkness, and clearly this cannot be done by preaching alone. The sermon cannot banish despair and grief. This calls for intense prayer and personal work. At the same time the sermon has its place in helping to point to the darkness which is beyond formulation and verbal expression. The disintegration which occurs is a necessary part of that turbulence which provides the basis of a shift towards the new. Over fifty years ago John Middleton Murry suggested that 'the church fails in leadership because it shows no sign of having known despair'.[4]

Christ comes to us as light in the darkness of the city, comes to 'light the dark streets'. The eucharistic readings for the fifth Saturday in Lent (Ezekiel 37: 21–28; John 11:45–56) have a common theme of gathering. God will gather his people from every quarter and they will never again be 'two nations' (Ezekiel 37:21–22). Jesus dies so that the whole nation might not be destroyed, but also to gather into one all the scattered children of God (John 11:50–52).

How can we proclaim this gospel in Britain and the USA where the reality of 'two nations' is all too evident? How can the destruction of these nations be averted and a covenant of peace (Ezekiel 37:26) be restored? Only by recovering the potential of the cross to unite across barriers, to overcome the darkness of division, can our preaching be relevant and a source of healing for all God's children.

Here then it is important to return to that misused theme of reconciliation. I suggested in an earlier chapter that reconciliation is often used cheaply, glibly and superficially. Yet while the noun and the verb are uncommon in the New Testament, and, apart from Matthew 5:24, occur only in Paul's writings, the theme is a vital one. The dark night is a prelude to the light of resurrection. The gulf and abyss which the cross exposes in all its horror is not the end: the end is liberation, the breaking down of the division, the overcoming of the gulf. There are some key passages in the New Testament which need attention in any preaching of the effective power of the cross as a means to overcome alienation and darkness. Let me mention four passages in particular.

Romans 3:24–26 points to the gift of God's grace through Jesus Christ whom God put forward as a sacrifice of atonement by his blood. Yet the freedom which grace gives operates only through the sacrificial blood. Sacrifice precedes harmony and peace. Similarly in 2 Corinthians 5:18–21, we are told that God has reconciled us through Christ and given to us the *diakonia* of reconciliation. God was in Christ reconciling the world to himself and entrusting the proclamation of reconciliation to us. So the work of reconciliation is both a message (*logos*) and a ministry (*diakonia*). The theme of reconciliation, not only between human beings but of all things, occurs in Colossians 1. All things in the universe were created in Christ and he is the unifying force – 'in him all things hold together'. Through Christ in whom 'the fulness of God' dwells,

God has reconciled all things in earth and heaven through the blood of the cross (Colossians 1:15–20). Reconciliation then is about issues and structures beyond the human: it embraces the created order itself. Finally, we are told that those who had been 'alienated from the commonwealth of Israel', hopeless and Godless, have now been brought near through the blood of Christ. Christ is described as our peace who in his flesh has made us one, broken down the wall of division, and created a new humanity, reconciling divided groups in one body through the cross and thus producing peace (Ephesians 2:11–18). The struggle to make this unity and peace a reality in human society is thus part of the proclamation of the cross.

A pastoral ministry which is rooted in the way of the cross needs to take these texts very seriously. It needs to be a ministry 'under the blood', utterly dependent for its effectiveness and life on the power of the blood of Jesus. It needs to be a servant ministry, seeing the proclamation of reconciliation as something which goes on at all kinds of levels, including very obscure places and times. It needs to hold fast to the vision of unity of all things and people in Christ, even though the barriers and forces of opposition to that unity are formidable ones, and the darkness at times seems impenetrable and unchanging.

GOD OF DARKNESS AND LIGHT

In the darkness and desolation of the cross, God is known. 'When you have lifted up the Son of Man, you will know. . . .' One of the central features of the understanding of God in the Jewish and Christian tradition is its insistence that God cannot be known directly. Only the idols can be known directly. They can be looked at, objectified, brought under our control. They are the tame gods, the gods of the *status quo*, the gods who know their place, the gods whom all governments like to have around.

The true and living God is known only in the consuming fire of the burning bush, in the cloud of Sinai, in the terrible darkness of Calvary. Only by entering into this darkness can we come to know God and ourselves. Only by entering the darkness can we recognise the light which shines precisely for this darkness. It is a step out of security into 'the night sky of the Lord'. Only by staying with the darkness does it become aglow with the divine glory. Only by leaving false securities behind can we enter the freedom of Christ the liberator.

The spiritual message of Calvary is that there is no future in trying to evade the darkness. The preaching of the cross must lead to a profound interior encounter with the reality of the cross. Our lives must be crucified and we must enter the night of pain on the road to God. Only those who go through something of Calvary and of the descent into hell, not alone but in solidarity with Christ who has been there, can find that life which comes through deliverance from the captivity of the false self.

But the darkness is not absolute nor is it an end in itself. As we move closer to the heart of the mystery so does the darkness change to light. In T. S. Eliot's words, 'the darkness shall be the light, and
the stillness the dancing'.[5]

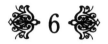 6

Christ Our Passover

Christ our Passover is sacrificed for us.
(1 Corinthians 5:7, King James Version)

It is important but curious to recall that, when we recite the threefold Holy followed by 'Blessed is he who comes' each day in the eucharistic prayer, we are repeating the words of the crowd on Palm Sunday, but doing so within the context of a song of awe to the God of all with whose glory the whole earth is filled (Isaiah 6:3). As Palm Sunday itself recurs, the name 'Holy' is given to the week which it inaugurates. It is in the midst of the strangeness and absurdity, the political turmoil and the dilemmas of discipleship, in the midst of darkness and desolation, that we encounter the holy. Only in the midst of worldly upheaval is the holy God known.

The uniquely Christian claim is that the cross is the focal point for the knowledge of God. Through the cross we are integrated into the life of God. We can say that the cross is the self-definition of God, the heart of the mystery of God's being. It is the centre of all faith and all theology. The preaching of the cross therefore cannot be marked by a sense of tragedy but only by a conviction of victory and liberation.

The passion narratives of the gospels set before us a messianic figure, moving towards his terrible destiny with a sense of triumph. From the first mention of the cross in Mark 8:31, there is a sense of inevitability but not of fatalism: he is to suffer, be rejected and killed, and rise again. Indeed he tells his followers that there are some standing there who will not taste death until they see that the Kingdom of God has come with power (Mark 9:1).

It is the supreme paradox, the ultimate folly, of the Christian proclamation, that the great feast of victory is known as Pascha, a word almost identical with that for suffering. Yet the Christian Pascha is celebrated in triumph. 'Christ our Passover has been sacrificed' is a shout of triumph. (In the Eucharist of the Episcopal Church of the USA it is shouted daily at the breaking of the bread.) To call Christ our Pascha, Paschal Lamb, is to identify him with the Passover, that great act of liberation of the people, achieved politically in the Exodus from Egypt, and expressed in the life of the community in the Year of Jubilee. To be a Christian at all is to live at Passover time.

To call the death on the cross Pascha is the most outrageously risky of all the Christian claims. It is to see in this death an act of liberation, of deliverance, of conquest of the forces of death and bondage. It is to assert, against all the evidence, that death is not the final word. And yet without death, resurrection can have no meaning.

To go to the apostolic preaching of the cross is to see how the cross is proclaimed as a symbol of victory. The word 'gospel' means 'good news', and it is as good news that the work of Christ is proclaimed. It is described as the good news of Christ (Philippians 1:27), the good news of God (Romans 1:1; 15:16), the good news of salvation (Ephesians 1:13), the good news of God's grace (Acts 20:24–25) and the good news of peace (Ephesians 6:15). It is good news because the cross is seen as a moment of victory. So in the Letter to the Colossians we are told that in the cross Christ 'disarmed the rulers and authorities and made a public example of them, triumphing over them in it' (Colossians 2:15). The sense of victory through the cross comes out strongly in the Book of Revelation where Christ is said to have freed us from our sins by his own blood and made us to be a kingdom (1:5–6). He is portrayed riding on a white horse with diadems on his head, clothed in a robe dipped in blood (19:11–13).

An important aspect of the New Testament teaching on the cross and resurrection is that Christ's victory is seen as our victory, and there is an emphasis on our solidarity in Christ, our participation in Christ. If the first portion of dough is consecrated, Paul tells us, so is the whole lump (Romans 11:16). Christ died in order to release life in us (1 Thessalonians 5:10).

THE UPLIFTING OF THE SON OF MAN

In the preaching of the cross we are lifting up the crucified Jesus before the eyes of people as a sign and source of life. The expression 'lifting up the Son of

Man' is a usage peculiar to John's Gospel, and there are three occasions in this gospel in which the Son of Man is said to be 'lifted up'. In 3:14, during the conversation with Nicodemus, Jesus prophesies that 'just as Moses lifted up the serpent in the wilderness, so must the Son of Man be lifted up, that whoever believes in him may have eternal life'. Here Jesus is being directly compared to the healing serpent who, in the Book of Numbers, is lifted up on a pole so that those who had been bitten by deadly serpents could look on the healing serpent and live (Numbers 21:4–10).

Then, at 8:28 there is a reference to the uplifting of the Son of Man within the context of revelation. 'When you have lifted up the Son of Man, then you will realise that I am he.' It is possible that there is here a direct allusion to the name of Yahweh, I AM. But whether this is so or not, it is clear that the author is linking the cross with insight and knowledge. It is only through this moment that people will begin to see clearly. The cross is a site of revelation about the nature of God in Christ.

Finally, at 12:31, the Son of Man is lifted up in the context of a cosmic conflict with the powers of evil. 'Now is the judgment (*krisis*) of this world; now the ruler of this world will be driven out. And I, when I am lifted up from the earth, will draw all people to myself.' Here the lifting up is seen as a site both of battle and of unity. The writer is saying that it is through the crisis of the world and its ruler that people will be drawn together.

One of the key themes of John's Gospel is the theme of glory. Jesus sees the cross itself as the moment of glory, the point at which the Son of Man is glorified.

In the passage from John 12 quoted above, Jesus announces that the hour has come for the Son of Man to be glorified, and he goes on to say that it is only when a grain of wheat falls into the ground and dies that it bears fruit (John 12:23–24). So his death is seen as a source of life and fruitfulness for all. The preacher who draws on John's account will emphasise the cross of Christ both as a source of life and light and as the supreme point of revelation of the glory and wonder of God.

During the Liturgy of the Passion on Good Friday we read the account of the passion from the Gospel of John. This is followed by the veneration of the cross and concludes with the reception of Holy Communion from the reserved sacrament. We can see in this liturgical celebration a threefold lifting up of Christ: in the reading of the words of the gospel; in the physical exaltation of the cross itself; and in the lifting up of the holy bread which has become his body for us. This liturgy is very powerful and speaks for itself, which means that often a sermon is not needed: the liturgy is the sermon.

But many churches find that it is useful to precede the liturgy with several hours of meditative preparation. The watch of silent prayer before the reserved sacrament on Maundy Thursday can be used as a time of corporate preparation for the liturgy of the following day. Word, silence, symbol and sacrament are all ways in which God is revealed, manifested and made real to us. It is in the exaltation of the cross as the tree of salvation and in the hymns associated with it that the Good Friday rite brings home to us the healing power of the cross.

'FAITHFUL CROSS, ABOVE ALL OTHER':
THE GLORY OF THE TREE

Over centuries both the visual symbols and the words associated with the cross have changed and have become more focused on the anguish, the blood and the wounds, and on personal contemplation of Christ's sufferings. But the earliest tradition was marked by a sense of triumph. The more ancient the crucifixes the more likely they are to show Christ as victor, as king, Christ in glory. Early crucifixes were of the Christus Victor type and reflected what is often called the 'classical' view of the atonement, in which Christ is seen as conqueror of the powers of evil. Many modern crucifixes have returned to the ancient type and show Christ in majesty, triumphant, with arms outstretched to draw all people to himself.

Similarly the more ancient the hymns the more likely they are to focus on victory and triumph. Venantius Fortunatus (535–609) wrote the hymn *Vexilla regis* which was traditionally sung as the office hymn at Vespers during the Passiontide season and is now sung at Evening Prayer in Holy Week. The hymn brings together wounding and conquest. Thus in the second verse the theme of piercing, taken from Isaiah 53:4 ('we accounted him stricken') and Zechariah 12:10 ('they look on the one whom they have pierced'), is fused with the ancient theme that the Church as a source of life and healing is born from the wounds of Christ.

> Where deep for us the spear was died,
> Life's torrent rushing from his side,

> To wash us in that precious flood,
> Where mingled water flowed and blood.

But then the hymn moves on to the theme of God reigning from the tree, based on Psalm 96:10 ('Say among the nations, "The Lord is king" ').

> Fulfilled is all that David told
> In true prophetic song of old,
> Amidst the nations, God, saith he,
> Hath reigned and triumphed from the tree.

The tree itself is then addressed as the source of salvation.

> O tree of beauty, tree of light,
> O tree with royal purple dight,
> Elect on whose triumphal breast
> Those holy limbs should find their rest.

At the Good Friday liturgy we sing Fortunatus' other great hymn *Pange Lingua*. This hymn has been part of the Good Friday rite since the ninth century. The singing of the hymn is linked with the veneration of the cross, which has been part of the liturgy of this day since the time of Egeria (c.380) whose account of Holy Week at Jerusalem is the oldest such document we have. In Egeria's time the revering of the *sanctum lignum crucis*, the holy wood of the cross, seems to have been a personal affair, but by the seventh or eighth century it was part of the public liturgy. As the cross is lifted up, it is addressed as the source of our life and liberation.

Faithful cross, above all other,
One and only noble tree.
None in foliage, none in blossom,
None in fruit thy peer may be.
Sweetest wood and sweetest iron,
Sweetest weight was hung on thee.

It is in these ancient hymns in particular that the victory of the cross is most powerfully stressed. It is a cause of great joy and celebration.

Sing, my tongue, the glorious battle,
Sing the ending of the fray,
Now above the cross the trophy.
Sound the loud triumphant lay.
Tell how Christ, the world's redeemer,
As a victim won the day.

The theme of the two trees – the tree of death and the tree of life – is also taken up in the Preface of the Eucharist for the Triumph of the Cross.

The tree of defeat became the tree of glory; and where life was lost, there life has been restored.

'O MY PEOPLE ...'

However, anyone who preaches the cross today must be aware of the danger of an approach which is triumphalist in a bigoted and intolerant way. This is not a new danger. From the earliest years of the Christian era the anti-Jewish polemic has been present in the proclamation of the cross. The removal of anti-semitic elements from the Christian liturgy is an ethical and theological imperative of our generation who have witnessed, and to a large extent colluded with, the horror of Auschwitz and of the Holocaust. For it is clear that the Holocaust emerged out of the very heart of Christian Europe and was the culmination of trends in European culture and in Christian thought going back hundreds of years. After Auschwitz the preaching of the cross can only take place – as it always should – with deep penitence and humility.

The potentially (and often actually) anti-Jewish elements in the liturgy of Good Friday focus mainly on two areas. One is the reading of John's Gospel in which 'the Jews' can be seen to mean the Jewish people as a whole rather than a particular group of enemies of Jesus. The second is the use of the Reproaches, a traditional anthem which begins with the words 'O my people . . .'. The Reproaches originated in the Mozarabic Rite and entered the Roman Rite in the eleventh or twelfth century, assuming their final form in the *Missale Romanum* of 1474. Because they can be seen as anti-Jewish, the American Book of Common Prayer omits them altogether. The Book of Alternative Services of the Anglican Church of Canada, however, has adapted them in a sensitive and thoughtful way which makes it clear that the accusation of infidelity and sin belongs to the whole of humanity. In this version the Reproaches begin: 'O my people, O my church . . .' They include the following section:

> I grafted you into the tree of my chosen
> Israel:

and you turned on them with persecutions
　　and mass murder.
I made you joint heirs with them of my
　　covenants:
But you made them scapegoats for your
　　own guilt.[1]

Today, as Islam grows in the west, and as many
people in inner areas of British cities are Muslim, it is
of the greatest importance that Christians preach the
good news of Christ crucified with humility, gentleness
and love, not using the cross as a weapon, but bearing
witness to our belief that here was God's love and
compassion most clearly shown. Churches need to
spend much time in thought and prayer in looking at
how their witness, in word and in liturgical celebration,
can be set forth so that the 'offence' of the cross is not
confused with offensiveness against particular groups
of people or faith traditions.

FROM DARKNESS TO LIGHT:
THE MYSTERY OF HOLY SATURDAY

We call this Friday good because the new humanity is
forged only out of the brokenness of the cross. The
New Testament knows of no knowledge of God apart
from this breakdown and reshaping of humanity of
which it is the record: it is in the midst of this process
of reshaping that God is revealed. To be a Christian is
to share in that process which is Christ's dying and
rising. It is to be in solidarity with Christ in his death
and resurrection. This solidarity is brought about and,
when it is celebrated properly, dramatically manifested

in the liturgy of baptism. For in the ancient symbolism of baptism, the candidate goes down into the waters, symbolically going into the grave, and rises again with Christ to the new life of the resurrection. Because the liturgy of baptism is the main liturgical way in which the Church celebrates the death and resurrection of Christ, traditionally the place for baptism is during the Easter Vigil which should, if possible, be celebrated in the very early morning of Easter Day.

The vigil begins in total darkness, and a new fire is lit. From the fire the paschal candle, which represents the risen Christ, is lit and carried through the darkened church. As the priest lights the candle she says:

> May the light of Christ, rising in glory, dispel the darkness of our hearts and minds.

The Paschal Proclamation is then sung. It is a triumphant hymn of praise which begins on the note of rejoicing.

> Rejoice, heavenly powers! Sing, choirs of angels!
> Exult, all creation around God's throne!
> Jesus Christ our King is risen!
> Sound the trumpet of salvation!

As the liturgy proceeds, a series of scripture readings recount the story of salvation history. At the heart of the rite is the blessing of the font and the baptism, and the celebration culminates in the first Mass of Easter. The Easter Vigil is the greatest act of worship of the Christian year, and shows in microcosm the whole of what it is to be a Christian. It focuses particularly on the meaning of the cross and resurrection. It represents the ending and the climax of the Lenten season as this time of reflection turns into a time of excitement and immense joy.

The word 'solidarity' is a sloppily used word but an important one theologically, a key word in understanding our relationship with Christ through baptism. Its root is in the word 'solid'; it speaks to us of our original condition, our true nature, as a communion. Christ restores us to communion in his own disintegration and restoration, in his dying and rising. The rising is contained in the dying and in the descent into hell, into the world of darkness and cold. It is in fact in the imagery of the harrowing of hell that we see the most powerful expression of the coherence of death and resurrection; and it comes out best in the iconography and liturgy of the east.

'TRAMPLING DOWN DEATH BY DEATH'

The Eastern Orthodox ikon of the resurrection shows Christ in hell, bearing the cross in his left hand, trampling the gates of hades beneath his feet, while his right hand grasps the wrist of Adam and raises him up. On the right stands Eve and behind her are all the kings and prophets and other biblical figures. The theme has its origin in 1 Peter where it is said that Jesus went and preached to the spirits in prison.

In the Orthodox liturgy, hell is made to speak:

Today doth hades groaning cry. My might is sacrificed. The Shepherd is crucified and Adam raised. Those that I ruled I have lost. Those I devoured in

my power I have disgorged them all. The Crucified
has opened the graves and the power of death has
no avail.

The cry of victory reaches a crescendo and a dimension
of ecstatic joy in the chant which is repeated over and
over again in the Easter Vigil rite.

Christ is risen from the dead, trampling down death
by death, and upon those in the tombs bestowing
life.

What does it mean, this victory over death? William
Stringfellow says that his friend Anthony Towne had
already overcome the bondage to death before he actually died. He had suffered all that the power of death
could do and so transcended the suffering. Death no
longer held dominion over him.[2] In Stringfellow's
account there is a sense of quiet confidence. But it is
not always easy, and all who minister to dying people
recognise not only the sense of peaceful resignation,
but also that of the abandonment of concern, a different
kind of transcendence. Thus Paul Oestreicher, in his
encounter with Ulrike Meinhof of the Baader Meinhof
gang, says that there was a kind of spiritual surrender.
She had ceased to care whether she lived or died. But
was this the emptiness of a soul redeemed or the
vacuum of loss of meaning of the lost sinner? The
mystery was too deep.[3]

The Christian sense of victory over death is not a
lack of concern with the reality of death. Death is
the final enemy to be conquered. But we believe that
Christ has overcome the dominion of death, and so

resurrection faith is rooted in confidence and hope that we too will overcome. Yet it has only happened through the encounter with death on the cross.

PREACHING THE CROSS
WITH CONFIDENCE

The celebration of Good Friday is neither a sad memory nor a secure one. It is a Passover celebration, and that celebration is dynamic, a feast for pilgrims, for people on the move, on the way to their liberation. Only such people, people in motion, can keep the Passover.

It is on this day most of all that the preacher has the opportunity to proclaim the 'word of the cross' as a word of power. When Paul speaks of 'Christ crucified' (1 Corinthians 1:23) he does so within this context of proclamation. That word needs to be proclaimed with confidence, not with arrogance, but in the utter conviction that in this man on the cross lies the hope of all humankind.

The cross stands between human fallenness and human fulfilment, between dust and glory, between Eden and the new Jerusalem. And yet we know only too well that these are not different places: for sin and grace, hate and love, dust and glory, Eden and Jerusalem, go right through the middle of us and of our communities. Christ's cross meets us at that point of conflict of our own fragmentation and tension towards the new. It is at the point of our most profound brokenness, at the shaking of the foundations of our being, that Christ's cross becomes for us a symbol of hope for the reversal of the forces of death. In the words of John Donne:

We think that Paradise and Calvary,
Christ's Cross and Adam's tree, stood in one place.
Look, Lord, and see both Adams met in me.
As the first Adam's sweat surrounds my face,
May the last Adam's blood my soul embrace.

References

CHAPTER 1

1. John Saward, *Perfect Fools* (Oxford University Press, 1980).
2. This is the argument of William Empson, *Seven Types of Ambiguity* (Penguin, 1962 edition, first published 1930), pp. 226–33, and, although his interpretation of Herbert has been questioned, I find it convincing.
3. Nicolas Berdyaev, *The Fate of Man in the Modern World* (SCM Press, 1935), p. 124.

CHAPTER 2

1. Edith Sitwell, *Collected Poems* (Sinclair-Stevenson, 1993 edition), pp. 272–3.
2. Audre Lorde, *Sister Outsider* (Trumansburg, New York: Crossings Press, 1984), p. 171.
3. Robert J. Schreiter, *Reconciliation* (Maryknoll: Orbis, 1992), p. 37.
4. Jurgen Moltmann, *The Crucified God* (SCM Press, 1974).
5. This idea seems first to have been used by Horace Bushnell, *The Vicarious Sacrifice* (1866), pp. 35–6, and was later taken up by P. T. Forsyth, *The Person and Place of Jesus Christ* (Independent Press, 1909). However, there is an earlier use of a similar theme in F. D. Maurice, *The*

Doctrine of Sacrifice (Macmillan, 1854) where he speaks of 'a ground of sacrifice in the divine nature'. See A. M. Ramsey, *F. D. Maurice and the Conflicts of Modern Theology* (Cambridge University Press, 1951), p. 65.

6. Douglas John Hall, *Lighten Our Darkness: towards an indigenous theology of the Cross* (Philadelphia: Westminster Press, 1976), pp. 140–41.

7. William McNamara, OCD, *Mystical Passion: spirituality for a bored society* (New York: Paulist Press, 1977), p. 25.

   The language of the crucified and suffering God is not new. Ignatius of Antioch speaks of 'the passion of my God' and 'the blood of God'. Cyril of Alexandria and Gregory Nazianzen use similar terms, while the Armenian theologian of the sixth century David the Invincible speaks of the 'cross of God' and of 'God crucified'. Bede, in his *De Tempore Ratione*, cap 66, notes that in 'the 18th year of the Emperor Tiberius, God by his passion redeemed the world'. Later Luther speaks of God's passion, God's blood, God's death, while in this century the language has been used by Karl Barth, William Temple and Jurgen Moltmann. It was used particularly movingly in the poetry of G. A. Studdert Kennedy ('Woodbine Willie'). See his *The Unutterable Beauty* (Hodder & Stoughton, 1930). Jon Sobrino says that 'God himself is crucified' (*Christology at the Crossroads*, Maryknoll: Orbis, 1978, pp. 224–5). See also Eberhard Jungel, *The Doctrine of the Trinity* (Grand Rapids: Eerdmans, 1976), pp. 83–8: 'God's Passion'.

8. Edith Sitwell, op.cit., pp. 292–6.

9. Ibid., pp. 370–76.

10. G. A. Studdert Kennedy, *The Unutterable Beauty*, op. cit., p. 24.

11. Rowan Williams, *Resurrection: interpreting the Easter gospel* (Darton, Longman & Todd, 1982), p. 18.

12. Sheila Cassidy, *Light from the Dark Valley* (Darton, Longman & Todd, 1994), p. 64.

CHAPTER 3

1. John P. Meier, *A Marginal Jew: rethinking the historical Jesus*, Vol. 1 (New York: Doubleday, 1992). See also Burton L. Mack, *A Myth of Innocence: Mark and Christian origins* (Philadelphia: Fortress Press, 1988).
2. Conrad Noel, *Manifesto of Catholic Crusade* (1918; new edition, London: Archive One, 1970), p. 16.
3. John Howard Yoder, *The Politics of Jesus* (Grand Rapids: Eerdmans, 1972); Richard Mouw, *Political Evangelism* (Eerdmans, 1973); Jim Wallis, *The Call to Conversion* (Lion, 1982), pp. 28, 56, 132.
4. Enoch Powell, *No Easy Answers* (SPCK, 1973), p. 26; Margaret Thatcher, cited in *The Guardian*, 16th October 1984.

CHAPTER 4

1. John N. Collins, *Diakonia: reinterpreting the ancient sources* (Oxford University Press, 1990) calls much of the current use of *diakonia* into question.
2. A. S. Byatt, *The Game* (Penguin, 1983), p. 38.

CHAPTER 5

1. Alan Ecclestone, *The Night Sky of the Lord* (Darton, Longman & Todd, 1980); Jim Garrison, *The Darkness of God: theology after Hiroshima* (SCM Press, 1982).
2. Ulrich Simon, *A Theology of Auschwitz* (Gollancz, 1967), p. 124.
3. Ibid., p. 127.

4. John Middleton Murry in *Malvern 1941* (Longman, 1941, p. 197).

5. T. S. Eliot, *Four Quartets* (Faber, 1970 edition), p. 28.

CHAPTER 6

1. *Book of Alternative Services of the Anglican Church of Canada* (Toronto, 1985), pp. 314–16.

2. William Stringfellow, *A Simplicity of Faith* (Nashville: Abingdon Press, 1982), p. 39.

3. Paul Oestreicher, *The Double Cross* (Darton, Longman & Todd, 1986), p. 58.